$4.75

KARL R. ZIMMERMANN

The Remarkable GG1

By

KARL R. ZIMMERMANN

Quadrant Press Review 6

QUADRANT PRESS, INC.
19 West 44th Street
New York, N. Y. 10036
Phone (212) 490-1622

ISBN- 0-915276-16-X

Other Quadrant Press Review Titles:

No. 1 STREAMLINED STEAM (out of print)
By Eric Archer $2.95

No. 2 THE MILWAUKEE ROAD UNDER WIRE (out of print)
By Karl R. Zimmermann $2.95

No. 3 ERIE LACKAWANNA EAST
By Karl R. Zimmermann $3.95

No. 4 ACROSS NEW YORK BY TROLLEY
By Frederick A. Kramer $3.95

No. 5 TWILIGHT ON THE NARROW GAUGE
By Frederick A. Kramer $3.95

No. 7 MOTIVE POWER OF THE JERSEY CENTRAL
By Michael Eagleson $4.75

ON THE COVER: The eastbound *Broadway Limited* crosses the Delaware River at Trenton, N. J., in the late 1950's.

PAINTING BY GRIF TELLER

Prints of this painting are available from George Pins, 350 Fifth Avenue, New York, N. Y. 10001 at $5.00 plus 50c for postage and handling.

Limited Edition of 100, numbered and signed available at $25.00 Postpaid.
(Print size 18''x24'')

ALL PHOTOGRAPHS THIS SECTION: KARL R. ZIMMERMANN

GG1: A Personal Album

The engine terminal at South Amboy, N. J., on October 23, 1976. Scuffing through the years' accumulation of sand, dust, and cinders, I step over a jumble of uprooted ties and wade through chest-high weeds. I pass aging Conrail E7's and E8's, paint peeling to juxtapose Penn Central logo and New York Central oval, elsewhere to let a bright red keystone re-emerge. The diesels look old, worn, and decrepit.

In the electrified section of the terminal are a trio of GG1's on tiptoes, "pans" outstretched to touch the catenary—raised high for safety here, as is typically the case in terminal areas. Nos. 4872 and 4874, the first two "G's" in line, wear PC black, but now carry only ludicrously small "CR's" on their spacious sides. With the early morning sun glancing obliquely from the locomotives' skins, it's easy to see the image of the Pennsylvania Railroad keystone in outline, as well as the more recently obliterated Penn Central herald.

The third GG1, No. 4883, still wears the broad yellow stripe introduced in the 1950's, and the yellow teardrops on the marker lights. She bleeds keystone red on her flanks. In spite of cosmetic blemishes, the G's still look modern and powerful. Incongruous here amid the weeds, they stand at rest; I can look at them at my leisure, note their perfect contours and overall balance.

South Amboy. Nearly two decades earlier I had brought a fledgling interest in trains here

Facing page: G's wear Amtrak platinum mist at Colonia, N. J. (top left), New Jersey D.O.T. black on the fly-over at Waverly, N. J. (top right), and the Pennsy broad-stripe at Princeton Junction, N. J. (bottom). Right: D.O.T. motors, then under Conrail aegis, at South Amboy, N. J., in October 1976.

to feed on the fast-vanishing K4 Pacifics. I stood then in virtually the same spot in the upper yard as now, but pointed my camera down, toward the dusty K4's steaming next to the concrete enginehouse. The G's in those days were taken for granted and received but casual attention—a side dish only, not the main course. Most wore the twenty-year-old pinstripes that had recently begun to give way to a flashy broad stripe and oversized keystone. Some of the G's that frequented the Amboy engine terminal were painted Tuscan red, matching the coaches they pulled, but most were dark green. They mingled with their just slightly older predecessors, the P5a electrics—both "modified" (or streamlined) and box-cab.

Today the K4's are long gone, as are the Baldwin "Sharknoses" that replaced them. The P5, though only two years the GG1's senior, has been gone for a decade. The Pennsylvania Railroad itself is gone, and so is the Penn Central that replaced it. But the GG1's remain, still forwarding certain New York and Long Branch trains—now Conrail's "North Jersey Coast Service" run under the auspices of the New Jersey Department of Transportation—from New York City's Penn Station to South Amboy, where diesels take over for the run south to the beach communities.

For generations, anyone who grew up in New Jersey—as I did—and watched trains saw a lot of the GG1. Though I may not have consciously paid it much mind—nor exposed much film on it—the G was always there. Most of my rail journeys, long or short, were launched from Newark's high-level platforms. In would rumble a GG1—large, powerful, strident within the close confines of the deteriorating station at Market Street. For someone young, the experience of being on that high-level platform as it vibrated with the GG1's passage was exhilarating and just a little frightening.

Facing page: A few examples of the Pennsy's broad-stripe scheme — seen here at Princeton Junction, N. J. (top) — lingered into the Amtrak era, as on No. 929 northbound at Waverly (bottom). ***On this page,*** *a G yields to E7's at South Amboy shortly after the Penn Central merger (top), roars into Newark Station (bottom left), and poses in a Washington sunset at Ivy City (bottom right).*

Above: Behind No. 4932, The Broadway Limited *rolls across the stone arch bridge over the Delaware River on March 29, 1976. Facing page: In April of 1976, No. 4934 waits under the train shed at Harrisburg for the arrival of the* Broadway *from the west (top left). Years earlier, when the Pennsy's broad-stripe was the current paint scheme for the G's, an eastbound streaks through Highland Park, N. J. (top right). G's Nos. 906 and 916 show off the two standard Amtrak paint schemes as they lead the* Silver Meteor *into the Jersey Meadows.(bottom)*

Standing on the platform—"locations 2 and 3 for Pullmans"—I waited to go south on the *Silver Meteor* or *Florida Special;* west on the *Broadway,* bound ultimately for Salt Lake City, Denver, or San Francisco; to Philadelphia on a "Clocker" for a football game; to Princeton for college; honeymooning to Virginia on the *F. F. V.;* holidaying to New Orleans on *The Southern Crescent;* to Roanoke, aboard a through Pullman for No. 1, the Shenandoah Valley train from Harrisburg; or to South Amboy, hunting the last K4's.

The GG1's were veterans twenty years ago, when my generation first knew them. They had seen the transition from heavyweight rolling stock to the new lightweight streamliners. (Much later still, they would see these "conventional" lightweight cars replaced by endless tubes of "Amfleet"—and at the same time come face to face with their own demise.) The G's were born into the steam era, watched that pass, and then saw a whole generation of diesel power come and go. And at the approximate age of forty, they have had the ironic, bittersweet pleasure of seeing their replacements fall short of the standards they set.

Now the GG1's days are numbered. These extraordinary motors have been around for so long that the prospect of their departure seems unreal and unreasonable. Nonetheless, it is actual. As 1976 ended, the G's were doing relatively little work for Amtrak, holding down on a regular basis just the Harrisburg trains, though frequently appearing on *The Montrealer, The Southern Crescent,* the *Silver Star* (usually double-shotted), and a few New York-Philadelphia "Clockers." They still haul-

ed a good deal of freight for Conrail, and some passengers too, but the locomotives' mortality could no longer be ignored. Though the G's don't show their age in aesthetics or performance, no machinery can last forever, especially in the face of the intense demands of high-speed railroading in the Northeast Corridor.

It won't come this year, and almost certainly not even in this decade, but the day is in the offing when the last GG1 will be retired, when Raymond Loewy's triumphantly successful styling will live only in museum and book, when tales of moving twenty cars down the Pennsy's "Broad Way" at an even "100 per" will become legend. Now the GG1 is unequivocally on the list of endangered species, and it is sure to be watched in its waning years with an intensity and wonder it hasn't known since its early days of trial and triumph.

ALTOONA PUBLIC LIBRARY

GG1: The Remarkable Story

The GG1 was born of inauspicious season. The mid-1930's were sad years for American industry. The Depression gripped fiercely, and the nation's railroads by no means escaped the clutches of economic stagnation and disaster. The Pennsylvania, however, the self-proclaimed "Standard Railroad of the World," was still paying dividends and was pressing forward a mammoth electrification program on its eastern lines that by the end of the decade would encompass 2677 track miles, or 40% of all the electrification in the United States.

For that, a new locomotive was essential. By 1935, after years of experimentation, the Pennsy had selected one that would remain for decades the symbol of its passenger operations under wire: the GG1. Fast, powerful, sleek, efficient, it has proven almost ageless and seemingly indestructible. On order as 1935 began were 57 of these remarkable locomotives, based on a prototype delivered in August of 1934 by General Electric and Baldwin and carefully analyzed at the railroad's test track in Claymont, Del.

The GG1's and the far-flung electrified lines over which they raced—and still race today—were distinguished by an unprecedented excellence and scope. These qualities came naturally, as the Pennsy had had a long history of interest in electrification, beginning in 1895 with an experimental operation on its Burlington to Mount Holly branch. In the first decade of this century, the Long Island Rail Road and the West Jersey and Seashore Railroad—both PRR subsidiaries—installed third-rail, low-voltage d. c. electrification, and in 1910 the Pennsy's New York City terminal operations were electrified in this manner, making possible the magnificent Pennsylvania Station in Manhattan.

It was the Philadelphia area, however, that gave birth to the Pennsy's single-phase a. c. catenary electrification, under which the GG1 eventually ran. By the mid-Teens, suburban traffic was so dense at Philadelphia's Broad Street Station that multiple-unit electric operation was indicated to unclog the bottleneck. Since the New York, New Haven and Hartford had realized good success with a. c. operations—and since alternating current has far superior transmission characteristics—the PRR chose this mode rather than staying with the d. c. system used in New York. In 1915 the twenty-mile Main Line to Paoli, Pa., was electrified, and in the next fifteen years more and more catenary was strung over lines radiating from Broad Street Station: to Chestnut Hill and then Whitemarsh, Pa.; to Wilmington, Del.; to West Chester, Pa.; to Norristown, Pa.; and, finally, to Trenton, N. J., in 1930. These lines were plied exclusively by owl-eyed MP54 suburban multiple-unit coaches, which eventually numbered in excess of five hundred. Main-line freight and passenger service remained steam-hauled.

Something much larger than the suburban elecrification was by this time already in the works, however. In October of 1928, the year the wires reached Wilmington, PRR president William Wallace Atterbury announced a main-line electrification project extraordinary in its dimensions; it was, in fact, the most extensive in railroad history. Catenary would be extended northward all the way to New York City, thus eliminating the need for the third-rail d.c. operation under the Hudson River from Manhattan Transfer in New Jersey to Penn Station in New York. Passenger trains would be able to run through from Penn Station all the way to Wilmington or Paoli without a locomotive change. Having long considered it, the Pennsy was now committed at last to main-line electrification.

Work on the project was barely under way when the Depression struck. President Atterbury and the PRR directors refused to be intimidated, however. Rather than pulling back, the Board in April of 1931 approved the southward expansion of the project to reach Washington's Union Station and, for freight, Potomac Yard, across the river in Alexandria, Va.

This electrification and improvement project—with an estimated cost of $175 million—was to include much more than hanging wire over 224 route miles of track. Just to adjust clearances to accept the catenary required the enlarging of tunnels and the raising of bridges in countless locations. At Baltimore, a double-tracked bore was added to the Union Tunnel. All along the line the track itself was upgraded, with some realignment, extensive reballasting, and the introduction of heavier rail. In the Elizabeth, N. J., area, the number of tracks was expanded to six, thus creating the broadest spot in the Pennsy's "Broad Way."

Stations too were a part of the program. The elimination of Manhattan Transfer in the Jersey Meadows as a power change point led to the construction of a new passenger facility in the area, the substantial station at Market Street in Newark. This $20 million structure, which also would serve the city subway, buses, and the Hudson and Manhattan "tube" trains, was opened for PRR use in 1935. Philadelphia's 30th Street Station—also new with the electrification—had been completed in 1933. (Its colonnaded grandeur remains virtually undiminished today, while the Newark

GG1 predecessors: A "modified" P5a leads a box cab. DON BALL, JR.

station has declined markedly.)

In spite of the Depression, the main-line electrification went into service bit by bit. The New York Terminal third-rail operations from Sunnyside Yard in Queens to Manhattan Transfer were converted to catenary; M. U. service with the ubiquitous MP54's was instituted from New York to New Brunswick, N. J.; trains began running through from Wilmington to New York behind electric power. Finally came the big event, on February 10, 1935: the initiation of through electrified passenger service from Washington's Union Station to Penn Station in New York. For this festivity, appropriately, the GG1 was on hand.

No locomotive design springs miraculously full-blown from nowhere, least of all one as surpassingly excellent as the GG1. Ever since commiting itself in 1915 to 11,000-volt, a. c. catenary on the Philadelphia-Paoli Main Line, the Pennsy had been looking ahead to comprehensive main-line electrification—and the locomotive that would make it work. Experimentation toward the development of such a projected paragon began with the 1-C+C-1 FF1 in 1917. This side-rod freighter, designed for heavy hauling at low speeds, was created with eventual electrification over the Allegheny Mountains in mind. "Big Liz," as the massive FF1 came to be known, was never duplicated but worked for more than twenty years boosting freight up the Philadelphia-Paoli grade.

Next in the design evolution came the 1-B+B-1 L5 in 1924. It was visualized as a "universal" locomotive, which could serve an entire railroad in both freight and passenger service with nothing more than gearing changes. A pair of L5a locomotives—designed for 650-volt d. c. operations—went into service at the same time on the New York Terminal Division, and another ten followed in 1926. Like "Big Liz" and the 33 DD1's that had been working the Sunnyside Yard-Penn Station-Manhattan Transfer third-rail operation since 1910, the L5's were jack-shaft, side-rod locomotives. Yet to be developed was a motor sufficiently powerful yet small enough to fit on the axle between the driving wheels, thus freeing electric locomotive design from the impediment of side rods.

Such a motor finally came in 1927, a development of Westinghouse Electric, and it was in effect the green light the PRR needed for its plans to electrify the New York-Washington line. Soon prototypes of three classes of electric locomotive were under construction for the Pennsy, all utilizing these new motors and sharing a number of interchangeable parts: the L6, a 2500-horsepower, 1-D-1 freighter; the P5, 2-C-2, 3750-horsepower, for heavy passenger service; and the O1, 2-B-2, 2500-horsepower, for light-duty passenger work.

Of this trio of designs, the P5—represented initially by a pair of prototype locomotives—seemed the most promising, so much so that ninety P5a's were ordered. Like the L6's and O1's, the first P5a's were box cabs. However, following a 1934 grade crossing accident fatal to the engine crew, a streamlined center-cab design was introduced for safety on the last 28 P5a's on order. In this design, which featured ends tapered for crew visibility, the basic aesthetic of the GG1 was born.

When, in 1933, the P5a's inaugurated Philadelphia-New York electrified passenger service, they were not an unmitigated success. They proved not to have the power necessary for heavy consists; serious problems with cracking of driving axles developed; and unsatisfactory tracking at high speeds negated the schedule improvements expected to accrue from electrification. Clearly the ultimate locomotive was still to come, one that would pull more, faster, than the P5a.

H. L. BROADBELT

ROGER COOK

SMITHSONIAN INSTITUTION

"Rivets"

The prototype GG1—No. 4800, nee No. 4899—has proven remarkably rugged. In its first 25 years, "Rivets"—as the locomotive is informally known, due to its unique carbody construction—ran off 2,795,577 miles, and it has been going strong in the 18 years since. Pictured here are the various liveries the locomotive wore while running under Pennsy aegis.

FRED W. SCHNEIDER, III

MARTIN ZAK

Top left: On March 27, 1956, No. 4800 leads The Duquesne *westbound over Conestoga Bridge, near Lancaster, Pa.* JOHN J. BOWMAN, JR.

Bottom left: No. 4800 with The Colonial *at Loudon Park, Md., in 1937.* SMITHSONIAN INSTITUTION

Top right: A broad-striped "Rivets" near Metuchen, N. J., in 1961. GEORGE HIOTIS

Facing page: In the gaudiest of her many schemes—applied in 1976 by Conrail for the Bicentennial—No. 4800 works south at Peach Bottom, Md., on the Columbia and Port Deposit. TOM KELCEC

4800
CR

Top left: Raymond Loewy's original air-brush rendering of his proposed design. Top right: In March of 1935, the first order of GG1's takes shape. RAYMOND LOEWY COLLECTION

Bottom left: This was the classic paint scheme as Loewy conceived it, with sans-serif lettering. DON BALL, JR., COLLECTION

In spite of all the experimentation in electric locomotive design that the Pennsylvania Railroad had been doing for the previous seventeen years, the GG1 was really the bastard son of a New Haven Railroad father. A test track had been established at Claymont, Del. (not far north of Wilmington) to analyze the P5a's problems. To this facility the Pennsy brought a leased NYNH&H EP3a (a 2-C+C-2 box cab) for tests, which showed the New Haven locomotive to track far better than the P5.

The Pennsylvania Railroad brass were sufficiently impressed to order a prototype GG1 embodying the EP3's wheel arrangement, which featured articulation between two units, and weight and horsepower distributed over a large number of axles. But they also ordered the R1, a 2-D-2 locomotive which extended existing PRR practices: a rigid frame and relatively fewer driving wheels conveying weight and horsepower. The PRR—showing a usually justified and perfectly excusable pride in its own—assigned the number 4800 to the R1, while giving the GG1 4899. Pennsy men, it may be imagined, were not anxious to see their own locomotive development repudiated by an intruder from the New Haven. The two prototypes were delivered in August of 1934.

The GG1 won hands down in the series of trials conducted at Claymont. As a result, the R1 was never duplicated while the prototype GG1 (its number promptly swapped for the R1's) ultimately came to enjoy 138 siblings. The first came in an order for 57 placed in 1934, which *Railway Mechanical Engineer* called "one of the largest locomotive orders in the history of American railroading." This batch of G's cost approximately $15 million—about $250,000 apiece—financed through a Federal Public Works Administration loan. The 57 locomotives were produced jointly by General Electric, Westinghouse, Baldwin, and the PRR's own Altoona works, all of which had collaborated on the prototype's design—along with Gibbs & Hill, engineers for the whole electrification project.

The statistics for the GG1: 4620 continuous horsepower, but over 8000 short-term; a driver diameter of 57 inches; weight of 460,000 pounds; length of 79½ feet; maximum starting effort of 72,800 pounds; articulated construction; power furnished by six pairs of twin traction motors (one pair per driving axle); quill drive; 11,000-volt, 25-cycle, single-phase. The first 57 G's were geared for ninety miles per hour.

To the machine described by these specifications, a touch of

"One of the good memories of my life. . . ." When No. 4840, the first production GG1 to be ready for service, appeared at Wilmington Shops, Loewy immediately went down to take a look. He posed proudly for a portrait with his locomotive, which gleamed in the sunlight on that bright April day in 1935. RAYMOND LOEWY COLLECTION

genius was brought by Raymond Loewy, the noted industrial designer. Joshua C. Taylor, the Director of the National Collection of Fine Arts, has written in his forward to a catalogue of an exhibit of Loewy's work: "Raymond Loewy has been a great creator of public symbols. A hardheaded technician, he also deals in myth, the kind of myth by which society lives." Certainly the GG1 has been one of Loewy's most enduring public symbols. It was a milestone in railroad locomotive styling, and in Loewy's own career as well.

Born in Paris in 1893, Loewy came to the United States immediately following World War I. After working for a decade as a fashion illustrator, he began in the late Twenties what he has called "a one-man industrial crusade under the aegis of good taste." He became an industrial designer, working in a profession that he was instrumental in founding.

In 1934 Loewy went in search of work to Pennsylvania Railroad president Martin W. Clement bearing a letter of introduction from Stuart Symington, later a United States senator. By the time he went to the Pennsy, Loewy had restyled the Hupmobile and the Sears Coldspot refrigerator; his credentials were established. A brusque Clement gave Loewy the glamorless job of redesigning the trash cans in New York's Penn Station, perhaps with the intention of brushing him off. After successfully completing this mundane task, Loewy was awarded, as a second assignment, the styling of the GG1—or, more accurately, was invited to submit a proposal.

Forty-two years later, in 1976, Raymond Loewy recalled the circumstances: "They built one prototype of the GG1. It was entirely riveted, with overlapping metal sheets. So what I suggested right at the start was that they weld the entire body of the locomotive. I told them, why build this when we can do better, so they gave me a chance." Loewy made a clay model and did some renderings embodying his ideas for the locomotive's design.

"Brute force can have a very sophisticated appearance, almost of great finesse, and at the same time be a monster of power," Loewy has said in describing his conception. "That's what I tried to do. The GG1 was almost an understatement." The PRR saw things his way, after recovering from its initial shock at Loewy's radical suggestion of a welded shell, a technique more indigenous to the automotive than railroad industry. Draftsmen worked up the Loewy design, and a full-size model was eventually constructed at the railroad's Wilmington Shops. Loewy next made a few refinements directly on the model, then pronounced the design ready for production.

Streamlining was still in its infancy when Raymond Loewy went to work refining the 4800. The Union Pacific's M-10000 *Streamliner*—with a skin of riveted plates similar to the 4800's—had recently appeared, as had the Shotwelded Burlington *Zephyr*. The *Zephyr* lent its shovel-nose, shroud-like design to many other early streamlined locomotives, both diesel (Otto Kuhler's Gulf, Mobile and Northern *Rebel,* and Goodyear-Zeppelin's *Comet* for the New Haven) and steam (Kuhler's *Hiawatha* Atlantic and Norman F. Zapf's "Commodore Vanderbilt" Hudson, which introduced streamlining to the New York Central).

For his GG1, Loewy did something different. He was fortunate to be starting with a form that was already basically streamlined: symmetrical with its center cab, tentatively graceful with its contoured hoods, hollowed and tapered organically to allow visibility for the engine crew. This basic design had been introduced for crew safety in the final P5a order—the "modified" series—and was embodied in the GG1 and R1 prototypes.

Loewy's stroke of genius was the decision to weld the entire exterior into a single, sleek, unbroken shell, removing all rivets and the seams between the plates. In addition to constituting a huge cosmetic improvement, this smoothing of rough edges made the locomotive more sound aerodynamically and had the happy result of cutting manufacturing and maintenance costs. Beyond the welding, Loewy made relatively small but crucial alterations in the prototype's contours, particularly at the "shoulders," and changed or eliminated certain specific details. The air-intake grilles were restyled. The numberboard "bumps" that originally protruded atop the locomotive's noses disappeared, and the teardrop marker lights became more horizontal in design. (These two alterations were made to the 4800 itself, as well as its descendants.) The steps up the nose of the engine to the roof were eliminated from the production design, as were the baffles above the nose doors. All of these changes were in the direction of simplicity, sleekness, and grace. Most were small, and only the welding itself was revolutionary. Yet, taken together, they wrought an extraordinary improvement.

Then there was the matter of the striping. As originally delivered, prototype GG1 No. 4899 wore an awkward tangle of striping on its side and nose panels: static and confused in pattern, not flowing

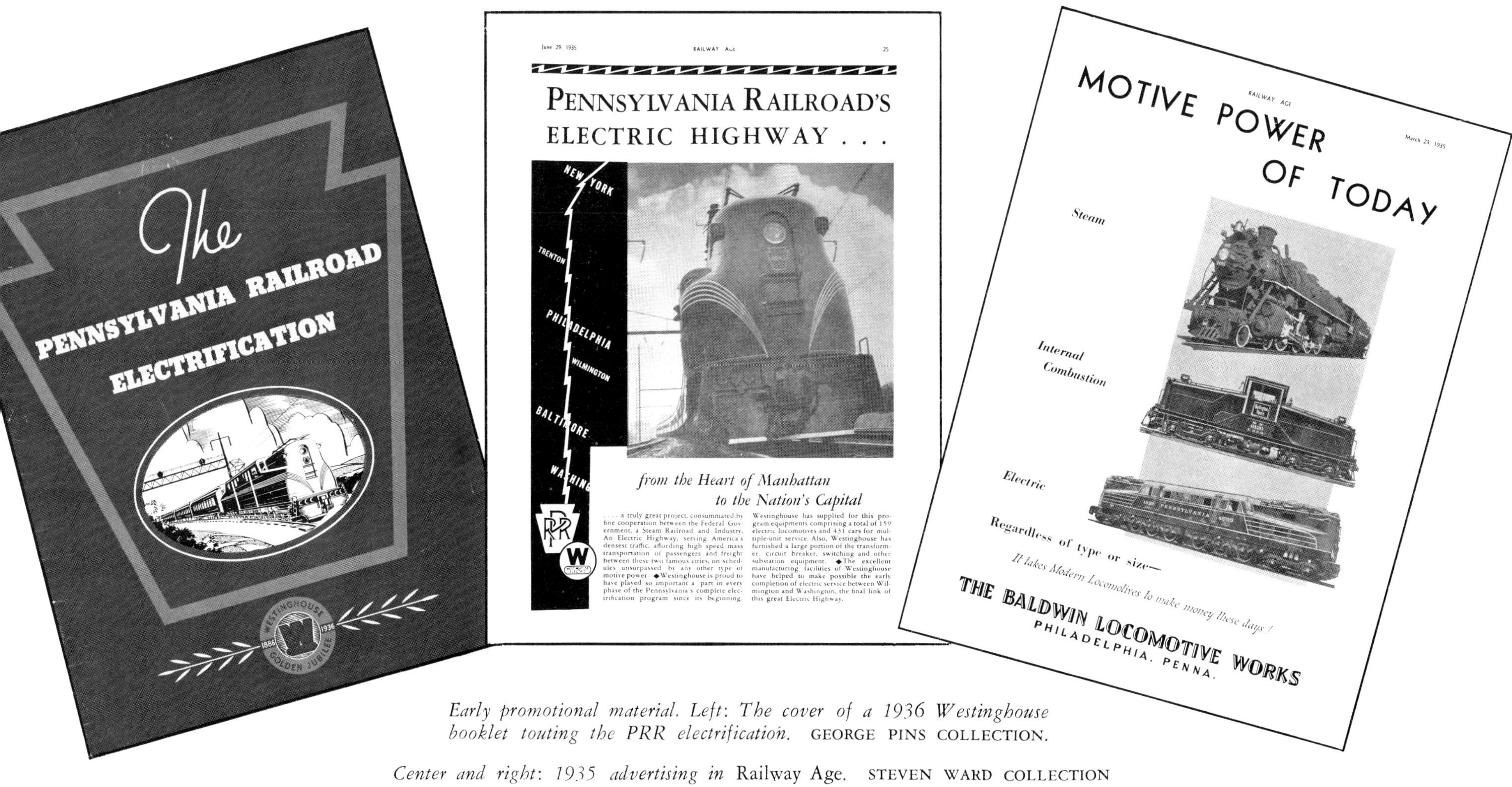

Early promotional material. Left: The cover of a 1936 Westinghouse booklet touting the PRR electrification. GEORGE PINS COLLECTION.

Center and right: 1935 advertising in Railway Age. STEVEN WARD COLLECTION

and simple. As part of his design concept, Loewy determined to replace this jumble with five narrow, elegant stripes in gold, which would run the length of the locomotive, then curve down over the nose to merge at the pilot, forming the distinctive, now-famous "cat's whiskers." In addition to aesthetic considerations, Loewy had a practical purpose as well for his design: "I decided to put gold stripes in front in a noticeable pattern so people working on the tracks would see that gold on dark green, which would stand out very well in critical light conditions." Loewy changed the lettering too. It had been bunched up; he stretched the word "Pennsylvania" all the way across the GG1's side, "to visually extend the length of the engine."

In the early weeks of 1935, all the GG1 collaborators were hard at work creating the various parts of the 57 locomotives that would embody Loewy's aesthetic. Meanwhile, electrified through-passenger service from New York to Washington was at hand. On January 28, a Washington-Philadelphia-Washington test run for government officials and other dignitaries was made with No. 4800. On that frigid day, with the temperature near zero, No. 4800 made the 134-mile southbound sprint in 110 minutes, including a stop at Baltimore, for an average speed of over 73 miles per hour. A portion of the run was made at 102 miles per hour—without seriously pressing the locomotive's potentialities.

Following this triumphant demonstration, No. 4800 and "modi-

fied" P5a No. 4780 went on a week-long display tour, which began on February 4. The locomotives were shown at New York, Newark, Trenton, Philadelphia, Wilmington, Baltimore, and Washington. The inaugural of New York-Washington service under wire came at the conclusion of the tour.

On the afternoon of February 10, from Washington Union Station and Pennsylvania Station in Manhattan, the *Congressionals* left behind electric locomotives—No. 4800 was on the northbound, No. 4780 on the southbound—thus beginning regularly scheduled electric service on this route. (The *Congressionals,* already long established as the premier trains on the run, were chosen very consciously for this honor. Always on the fastest schedules, through the years they have been the benchmark whenever operations on this line are discussed.) In June of 1935, freight trains began running under wire to "Pot Yard" in Alexandria, and the electrification project was complete—for the moment.

By then a number of sleek new GG1's were in service. No. 4840 had been the very first to arrive, one of four locomotives delivered in April. Raymond Loewy recounts his first glimpse of this initial GG1 as "one of the good memories of my life." He recalls being telephoned by the Pennsy's Chief of Motive Power Fred W. Hankins and Chief Engineer John V. B. Duer with the good news: "We have one of your babies finished. Do you want to come down to Wilmington and have a look?" Loewy did—and was satisfied. Though he went on to design countless hundreds of other objects, machines, vehicles, and buildings—most of them not in the railroad field—Loewy would still say, in 1976, "I have a special warm spot in my heart for the GG1."

By August of 1935, all 57 GG1's in the first order had been delivered and were running, and P5a's had begun to be re-geared for freight service. It was estimated in the March 1935 "Train Talks" (one of the small pamphlets on a wide variety of subjects issued periodically by the Pennsy) that 686 trains per day were operated under wire. Now that the electrification project could be evaluated, it was judged in all quarters to be a resounding success. As the somewhat melodramatic prose of "Train Talks" had it, "Like flying shuttles of a giant loom, great engines harnessed to the magic force of electricity now flash between the nation's capital and its largest city over ribbons of shining steel." Hard facts supported this whimsy: The *Congressional's* time was cut from 4¼ to 3¾ hours, and other schedules were similarly reduced. Later, in

LIONEL "0" GAUGE TRAINS

OUTFIT No. 2139W
$57.50
WITH BUILT-IN HORN

No. 2139W LIONEL FOUR-CAR FREIGHT SET

With Built-in HORN

Speed and power-plus are built into the strikingly realistic electric type Locomotive which heads this freight outfit. Patterned after famous Pennsylvania R.R. "GG-1" model, this Locomotive has pantographs which raise and lower and which can be adjusted to pick up current from overhead wires. Lumber car unloads by remote control. Train set is 4 ft., 1½ in. long. Track forms oval 61 inches by 31⅞ inches.

Outfit consists of: 1 No. 2332 Pennsylvania Electric-type Locomotive with built-in Horn—1 No. 3451 Operating Lumber Car, with load of Logs—1 No. 2458 Automobile Car—1 No. 2456 Hopper Car—1 No. 2357 new illuminated Caboose—8 sections OC Curved Track—5 sections OS Straight Track—1 RCS Track Set—1 CTC Lockon—1 Tube of Lionel Lubricant—1 No. 926-5 Instruction Booklet. $57.50

Magnificent LIONEL GIANTS OF THE RAILS

OUTFIT No. 2144W
$67.50
WITH BUILT-IN HORN

No. 2144W LIONEL "O" GAUGE THREE-CAR DE LUXE PASSENGER OUTFIT

With Built-in HORN

Real Pennsylvania R.R. trains like this carry millions of people each year between such cities as New York, Philadelphia and Washington. This all-Pullman special is built to pound along at high speeds with effortless ease. Twenty-wheel Electric type Locomotive has deep-toned Horn and pantographs that raise and lower. Illuminated passenger cars have 6-wheel trucks, inset windows, doors that open and shut. Train is 4 ft. 11 in. long. Track furnished forms oval 61 inches by 31⅞ inches.

This magnificent train set includes: 1 No. 2332 Pennsylvania Railroad electric-type Locomotive with built-in realistic Horn. Authentic pantographs raise and lower and can be adjusted to draw current from overhead wires. Loco has 20 wheels, including 12 powerful drivers—1 No. 2625 "Irvington" Pullman with interior illumination—1 No. 2627 "Madison" Pullman with full inside lighting—1 No. 2628 "Manhattan" Pullman with interior illumination—8 sections of OC "O" Gauge Curved Track—5 sections of OS "O" Gauge Straight Track—1 RCS remote control Track Set—1 CTC Lockon—1 Tube of special Lionel Lubricant for locomotives—1 No. 926-5 illustrated Instruction Booklet. $67.50

Facing page, top: In its first year of service, No. 4800 departs from Washington Union Station. H. W. PONTIN, HERBERT H. HARWOOD, JR. COLLECTION

Facing page, bottom: No. 4810 swings through the old Dillersville curve, which has long since been realigned. WILLIAM M. MOEDINGER, JR.

Above: The wide appeal of the GG1 was attested to by the great popularity of the famous Lionel model of the locomotive, which commanded the centerspread of the 1948 catalogue. BRUCE GREENBERG COLLECTION

Right: Less widely known than the Lionel model was a cardboard cutout GG1, designed by British artist Wallis Rigby, who is shown here handing his model to a 12-year-old John B. Gambling, Jr., while John B. Gambling, Sr., looks on. First the father and then the son have been mainstays of New York City radio for decades with their early-morning "Rambling with Gambling" program. The Gamblings were treated to a ride aboard a full-sized GG1. Millions of Rigby's cardboard cutouts of locomotives, airplanes, and ships were sold in England.
A. F. SOZIO, THEODORE F. GLEICHMANN, JR. COLLECTION

April of 1936, the *Congressional's* schedule would be slimmed again—to 3 hours and 35 minutes.

Schedule reductions of this sort were made possible by the GG1's remarkable acceleration and its ability to take grades in stride without reducing speed—characteristics that resulted from the short-time overload capacity of electric motors. These shortened schedules had the important effect of expanding the capacity of existing trackage, one of the major goals of the electrification. Another plus wrought by electrification of lines as densely trafficked as the Pennsy's was economy through centralized power generation. Power generation facilities at stationary, lineside plants could in effect do three times the work of prime movers aboard locomotives (diesel-electrics) through averaging of demand. Locomotives idle or running downgrade drew no power; only a relatively small percentage of the locomotive fleet would be accelerating or running upgrade at any given time; therefore, through centralization, a substantially smaller generating capacity would suffice. So the electrification and the GG1's allowed the Pennsy to run more trains, and to run them faster and more cheaply.

The Pennsy's 1934 Annual Report found the electrification project to exceed "in magnitude and importance that on any other railroad in miles of track electrified, in volume and density of traffic handled, in number of trains affected, and terminal operations involved." Furthermore, the project was a social as well as operational success. In early 1934, the PRR had borrowed funds from the Public Works Administration—money eventually used to buy the GG1's and press forward the entire program. Looking back, the Administrator of the PWA characterized the loan to the PRR as the most productive ever made by the agency. It created an estimated 45,000,000 manhours of work for PRR employees and for the manufacturers of materials and equipment used on the project and put to work about 25,000 men who otherwise would have been idle.

What does success breed but the desire for more of the same? To realize full economies, the PRR had to extend the wires, for the secret of electrification is volume. On January 13, 1937, the Pennsylvania Railroad's Board of Directors formally authorized further electrification, this time to the west. It was to comprise the Paoli-to-Harrisburg main line, the low-grade freight line to Enola, Pa. (the Atglen and Susquehanna), the Columbia Branch, the Trenton Cutoff and Philadelphia and Thorndale Branch (from Morrisville to Thorndale, Pa.), and the Columbia and Port Deposit line up the Susquehanna River from Perryville, Md., to Columbia, Pa. The line from Monmouth Junction to Jamesburg and South Amboy, N. J., was also included. All together this would total 315 route miles and 773 track miles.

This called for more GG1's, and at least a few arrived every year from 1937 through 1943, when a grand total of 139 locomotives was reached. Beginning with the 1937 "motors" (as electric locomotives were inevitably called by Pennsy railroaders), the GG1's were delivered with rounded drop-coupler cast-steel pilots and 100-mile-per-hour gearing. Otherwise, they were identical to the original 57. Of that original order, 14 locomotives had been built entirely by General Electric; 25 more had been built by tripartite arrangement involving Baldwin, the Pennsy's Juniata Shops in Altoona, and either Westinghouse or GE. The remaining 18 locomotives in that first order were built by just the PRR and either GE or Westinghouse, as were the 82 additional GG1's which came later.

The first electric-powered passenger train entered Harrisburg on January 15, 1938. It was the westbound *Metropolitan* for Pittsburgh, and GG1 No. 4863—a brand-new Altoona product—was on the point. Now, as far as passenger service was concerned, the "loom" of electrification was complete. The "shuttles"—or passenger trains—that flew across it were phenomenally numerous. At first they were all in the "heavyweight" mode, but at the five-month anniversary of the Harrisburg electrification's opening that changed dramatically.

On June 15, 1938, the "lightweight," streamlined "Fleet of Modernism" was introduced with the inauguration of an all-new *Broadway Limited* on a 16-hour New York-Chicago schedule—an unprecedented timing, made possible in part by the GG1. The lightweight *Broadway*—which was put in service simultaneously with a streamlined *20th Century Limited* on the New York Central—was styled inside and out by Raymond Loewy, now on a long-term retainer with the PRR. He was also responsible for the balance of the "Fleet of Modernism," introduced shortly after the *Broadway*: *The General* (also New York to Chicago), the *Liberty Limited* from Washington to Chicago, and the *"Spirit of St. Louis"* from New York and Washington to St. Louis. Though the Washington trains, which ran north to Harrisburg on the non-electrified line through York, Pa., were handled by G's only as far as Baltimore,

A Multitude of Trains

Right: *No. 4831 waits while* The Congressional *loads its passengers at Washington in 1935.* H. W. PONTIN, HERBERT H. HARWOOD, JR. COLLECTION

Below: *In March of 1937,* The Congressional *glides through Loudon Park, Md.* SMITHSONIAN INSTITUTION

Left: *In two March 1956 views showing heavy head-end business,* The Admiral *climbs east near Gap, Pa. (top), and the westbound* Metropolitan *swings into Bradford Hills curve, just past Downingtown, Pa.* JOHN J. BOWMAN, JR.

Above: *Loewy's 1938 "Fleet of Modernism"* Broadway Limited *makes a preinaugural run behind No. 4892.* ALTOONA PUBLIC LIBRARY

Facing page: *Nearly 27 years later the* Broadway *is still all-Pullman and all right as it sweeps eastbound through Colonia, N. J.* PETER TILP

4882
4882 PENNSYLVANIA

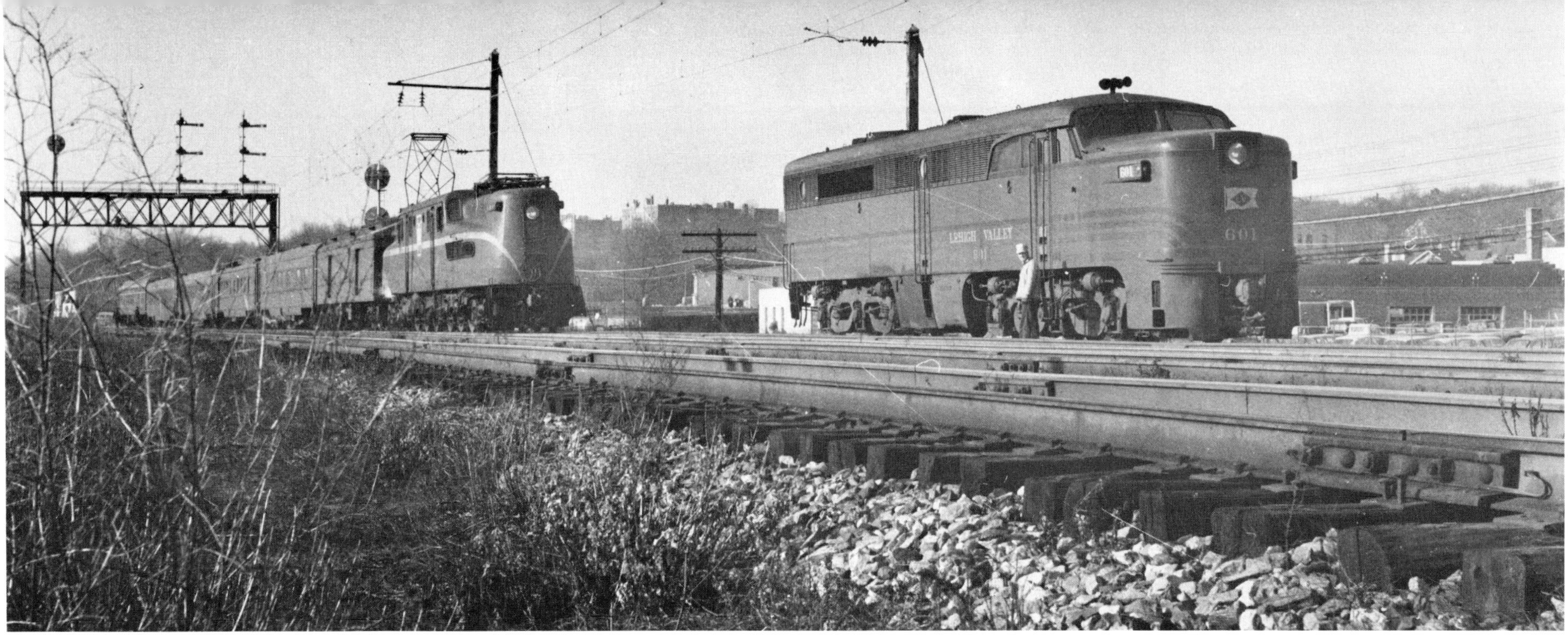

4897
PENNSYLVANIA
4897

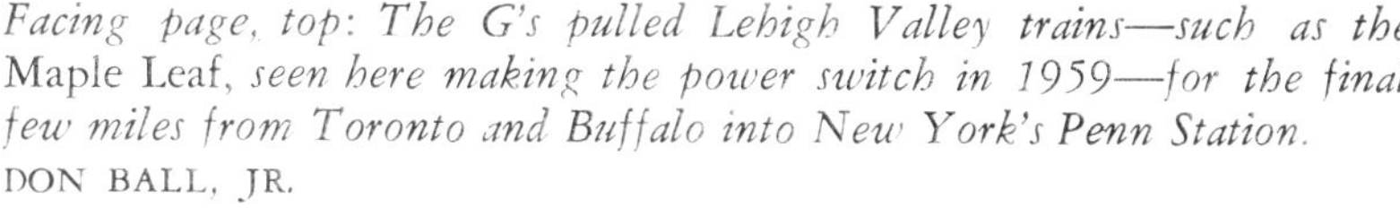

Facing page, top: The G's pulled Lehigh Valley trains—such as the Maple Leaf, *seen here making the power switch in 1959—for the final few miles from Toronto and Buffalo into New York's Penn Station.*
DON BALL, JR.

Facing page, bottom left: The Mount Vernon *at New Brunswick, N. J.*
VICTOR HAND

Facing page, bottom right: The Juniata *at Elizabeth, N. J.*
ROBERT R. MALINOSKI

Above: G's in Sunnyside Yard in Queens await assignment.
HOWARD SERIG

Top right: Pennsylvania Limited *at Lancaster, Pa.* FRED W. SCHNEIDER, III

Bottom right: A local from the New York and Long Branch.
GEORGE HIOTIS

Top left: A Florida train in the heavyweight era.
RAYMOND LOEWY COLLECTION

Bottom left: The Atlantic Coast Line's Champion *crosses the Schuylkill River in Philadelphia.*
DON BALL, JR.

Above: The Silver Meteor, *a Seaboard train, roars through Arbutus, Md., in 1964.*
HERBERT H. HARWOOD, JR.

Facing page: Florida service, Amtrak style, at Havre de Grace, Md., in May of 1976. TOM KELCEC

the New York trains in the "Fleet" were electric powered all the way to Harrisburg. The sleek GG1's seemed at home on these new streamliners, whose tasteful appearance had sprung from the same font of creativity as their own.

The following year brought another addition—the luxury, all-coach *Trail Blazer* from Chicago to New York. This train, made up of rebuilt and modernized cars, proved so popular that within two years a similar service was installed on the St. Louis-New York line: *The Jeffersonian.* From Harrisburg east the G's supplied the power, taking whatever length consists seasonal demand could throw at them—consists of up to twenty cars and more—and running them home on the advertised.

The glamorous "Fleet of Modernism" was only a small piece of all the passenger business for which GG1's were responsible. On the line to Harrisburg were such additional services as these: *The Golden Arrow, The Rainbow, Pennsylvania Limited, Manhattan Limited, Gotham Limited,* and *The New Yorker* for Chicago; *The Akronite, Cincinnati Limited,* and *The Clevelander; The Red Arrow* for Detroit; for St. Louis, *The American* and *The St. Louisan;* for Pittsburgh, *The Juniata, The Metropolitan, The Duquesne, The Iron City Express,* and the all-room *Pittsburgher.*

On the north-south route to Washington, the flagship was *The Congressional.* Keeping it company in the years when the GG1's were young were such New York-Washington trains as *The President, The Edison, The Judiciary, The Representative, The Legislator, The Embassy, The Constitution, The Potomac, The Arlington, The Mount Vernon,* and *The Admiral* (which became a New York-Chicago train during World War II). *The Patriot, The Federal, The Colonial,* and *The Senator* continued on to Boston via the New Haven's Hell Gate Bridge route, in many cases behind the EP3 box cabs that figured in the development of the GG1. On the Philadelphia-Boston run, they were joined by *The Pilgrim, The William Penn,* and *The Quaker. The Montrealer/Washingtonian* pair ran behind GG1's on the southern leg of their travels.

Pennsy G's handled as far as Washington a myriad of through trains from New York City to points south, either combined with PRR trains or as separate consists. For the Atlantic Coast Line, GG1's at one time or another forwarded the *East Coast Champion, West Coast Champion, Florida Special, Vacationer, Everglades, Havana Special, Palmetto,* and *Miamian;* for the Seaboard Air Line, *The Orange Blossom Special, The Camellia, The Cotton Blossom, The Palmland, The Sunland,* and the *Silver Meteor, Silver Comet,* and *Silver Star.* The Chesapeake and Ohio's *Sportsman, F. F. V.,* and *George Washington* began their runs behind GG1's, and the Southern's *Crescent, Southerner, Peach Queen, Asheville Special, Tennessean, Pelican, Birmingham Special,* and *Piedmont Limited*

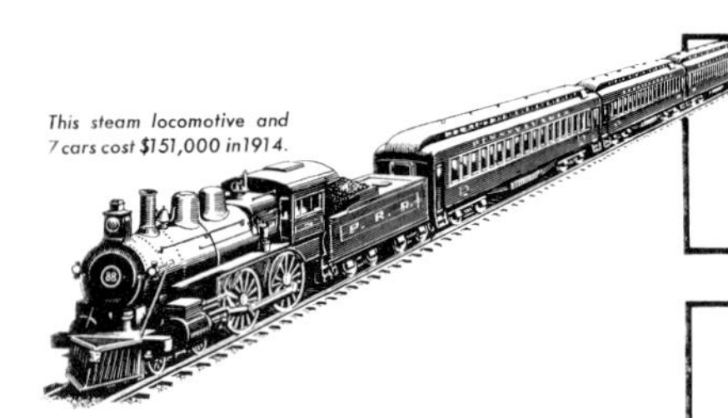

1914 MAGNIFICENCE

Brand new equipment costing a hundred and fifty thousand dollars made its proud debut. Again "The Congressional" set new standards for travel comfort. *"Sorry about the cinders, lady, let me brush you off."*

1952 LUXURY

Thirty-eight years of progress in making Pennsylvania trains faster, safer and more comfortable reached a new peak of luxury in the 1952 Morning and Afternoon Congressionals—christened March 17th, 1952. *As one newspaper said "The New Congressionals—WOW!"*

This electric locomotive and 18 cars cost $3,224,000.

How can Railroads afford such luxury?

THE SECRET of the Pennsylvania's beautiful new trains is plenty of pleased passengers.

Over a million people a year will enjoy the luxuries of a fine hotel lounge as they ride the Morning and Afternoon Congressionals between New York, Philadelphia and Washington. There is plenty of space aboard for 700 passengers to relax, read or dine as they choose—and nearly every seat is being taken nearly every trip.

Such patronage deserves the best and the Pennsylvania is glad and proud to provide it—to invest nearly $5,000 for the accommodations for each passenger—because travel on these trains justifies the investment.

Meanwhile, on some little-traveled lines we are required by law to continue running trains that almost no one wants. Antiquated equipment that pleases no one—least of all the railroad men who operate it at a loss—runs nearly empty on most days. (Last year this railroad was denied permission to cease operating a train which carried an average of 24 passengers. During February, 1952 the patronage was down to an average of 16 passengers per trip. Railroad progress where needed is thwarted by the losses resulting from such "horse and buggy" regulation.)

Given the freedom to operate its railroad business under the incentives of competitive enterprise, the Pennsylvania will be glad to provide the best possible service wherever patronage offers business opportunities.

Isn't this what most Americans want?

PENNSYLVANIA RAILROAD

Go by Train . . . In Safety and Comfort

Ad No. 3P-6528-Final
United States News, April 25, 1952

This ad from April 1952 features a red GG1, pink cherry blossoms, a brand-new stainless-steel Congressional, *and a knock at government regulatory policies.* GEORGE PINS COLLECTION

did the same.

This extraordinary list is suggestive rather than definitive. It omits, for instance, the frequent New York-Philadelphia "Clockers," numbers of other nameless trains, and some named trains as well. It conveys dramatically, however, the way in which 139 GG1's were busy around the clock, racing passenger trains across the wishbone New York-Philadelphia-Harrisburg or -Washington main lines of the PRR. In 1939, the Pennsylvania Railroad was dispatching an incredible 3500 passenger trains daily. A great number of them served New York's Pennsylvania Station where, between seven and ten o'clock in the morning, a train would arrive or depart once a minute. Though this included Long Island Rail Road and New Haven Hell Gate services, plus the PRR's own MP54 M.U. schedules, a great many of that extraordinary eruption of trains—which numbered more than 900 a day—were headed by GG1's.

The G's pulled everything in sight. They were strong enough to handle the heavyweight consists that provided all the passenger service in their early years; they were sleek enough to match the streamliners, beginning with the "Fleet of Modernism" in 1938. In 1939 the *Champion* and *Silver Meteor* were added to the GG1 streamliner count; in 1941 *The Southerner* and *The Tennessean* continued the trend. By this time other Pennsy trains began to get lightweight equipment, and a new era had arrived.

World War II, which temporarily halted the influx of lightweight equipment, was perhaps the GG1's finest hour. The Pennsy's electrified service, linking the nation's most important cities, met unprecedented travel demands with frequent extra sections and consists that routinely ran in excess of twenty cars. Since motive power was at a premium, GG1's handled even the heaviest trains without doubleheading. Materiel, troops, military brass, and legislators—all moved behind the G's, whose speed, power, and high availability kept the corridor unclogged.

After the war, the trend to streamliners continued. In 1952, when the Pennsy introduced with much ballyhoo its new *Morning* and *Afternoon Congressionals*—eighteen-car deluxe trains, built by The Budd Company and featuring twin-unit diners, seven-room conference parlor cars with telephone, and parlor-buffet lounge-observations—the company did not hesitate to spotlight the GG1 in its advertising. Loewy's 17-year-old design still looked perfectly contemporary and absolutely appropriate to lead Budd's new stainless-steel consists. (The Washington-Boston *Senator* was similarly re-equipped at the same time, though in slightly more modest fourteen-car length.) The G's also powered the *Keystone* consists, Budd's tubular, low-center-of-gravity trains introduced in 1956.

Another kind of passenger operation, and a spectacularly impressive one, was the Army-Navy football specials the Pennsy ran to Municipal Stadium in Philadelphia. These began in 1936 and for forty years remained predominantly the province of the GG1. Each year the specials were an extraordinary undertaking—the "most concentrated passenger train operation in the United States" according to the PRR. In 1936 there was a total of 38 trains. The record number was 42, in 1941; this included not only the usual service from New York and Washington, but also a single consist from Atlantic City. The war intervened, and for three years there were no Army-Navy games at Municipal Stadium. In 1945 the special trains resumed with a modest total of eight, but in 1946 the number jumped to 37 and the tradition was hale again.

The November 27, 1954, trains—when the specials were still thriving—were chronicled in *The Pennsy Magazine*, an employee publication. That day, 29 special trains with consists totalling more than four hundred coaches, Pullmans, and diners converged on Greenwich Yard, adjacent to Municipal Stadium, and all arrived on time. Among the 20,470 passengers that the Pennsy brought to the game that day were the 2500-strong corps of Cadets from West Point and a trainload of senators, congressmen, and Supreme Court justices. This 29-train move had been nine weeks in preparation. In addition to on-train crews, it involved at Greenwich 20 ushers, 44 coach cleaners, and 43 PRR policemen to insure the safety of boarding and detraining passengers as the GG1's moved in and out among the dozen platforms.

Year after year, coming from New York City and the north, GG1's would lead their specials off the main line at Zoo tower, proceed along the West Philadelphia Elevated Branch past 30th Street Station and the University of Pennsylvania's Franklin Field (to which the Pennsy also ran football specials), then switch at Arsenal tower to the Delaware Extension for a four-mile run to Stadium tower and Greenwich Yard. Trains from the south also approached via Arsenal. Even after Greenwich Yard was expanded during World War II, some sections had no catenary; since this space was needed for train parking, the practice was for the GG1's to coast, with "pans" down, past the "A. C. Motor Stop" indications

Above: The GG1's longevity is underlined by the ease with which the motors outlasted such ill-fated experiments as the Aerotrain, *seen here on display in Lancaster, Pa., in January 1956.* FRED W. SCHNEIDER, III

Below: G's also pulled the more successful Keystone, *shown here at Iselin, N. J., in 1967 in a mixed consist with conventional equipment.* PETER TILP

The Army-Navy Specials

Army-Navy Specials at Municipal Stadium in Philadelphia in the heavy-weight era. Facing page, top left: DON BALL, JR. *Facing page, bottom and top right and above:* PETER TILP COLLECTION

Below and right: The Army-Navy operations in the pre-PC 1960's. PETER TILP

and out from under the wires. During the game, steam switchers hauled the G's out and placed them on the front of their trains.

The sheer density of traffic made each Army-Navy day a railroading epic to which the PRR could point with pride. There was nothing else quite like it, though GG1's also hauled smaller numbers of football specials to Princeton, N. J. These trains moved over the three-mile Princeton Branch (in local parlance inevitably the "PJ&B"—Princeton Junction and Back—as if it were a separate and mighty railroad) to the small stub-end yard across from the Princeton station. Since there was no passing track, one light GG1 would be dispatched to Princeton behind the specials. After the game, this G would couple on to the tail end of the first train scheduled to depart and take it out. This would free that train's original locomotive to couple on to the rear of the second train.

Even in Penn Central black the GG1's carried on the Army-Navy tradition. In 1968, four motors are visible in the line-up outside the stadium (top left). In the Amtrak era, GG1 No. 906 leads a special from New York along the "High Line" and past Philadelphia's 30th Street Station in 1973. PETER TILP

Facing page: A pair of G's lead a freight eastbound at Bush River, Md., on January 4, 1970.
VICTOR HAND

This procedure continued until all the trains were gone, leaving one light GG1 to follow along behind.

But Army-Navy day was a far more extensive and complicated operation, and one that featured quality as well as quantity. For one thing, a number of "POTUS" moves—involving the President of the United States—are part of Army-Navy-day history. The last president to arrive at the game by rail was John F. Kennedy, who in both 1961 and 1962 rode aboard PRR business car No. 120 to or from Municipal Stadium—which only a year later would be rededicated to bear his name in memoriam. In the great days of the specials, a profusion of office cars, private cars, and Pullmans converged from all over—making Greenwich Yard a temporary haven for train-watchers. Heavyweight parlors and section sleepers from the Pullman pool continued to appear into the 1960's.

Like all passenger service, however, the Army-Navy trains fell on hard times. In 1958, the first year that M.U. trains were used in the operation, there were still 27 specials in all. By 1962, however, the count was down to 18, including four M.U. trains—to Trenton, Wilmington, and Paoli. In 1975, the last year G's were involved, there were but two consists from New York—led by GG1's Nos. 926 and 906 in Amtrak's platinum mist, red, and blue—and two from Washington. In 1976, E60's and Amfleet cars took over, and there were two Washington trains and just one from New York. A grand tradition is apparently near its end. In an age of autos, few choose to ride the train.

Though they were designed as passenger locomotives, the GG1's have proven remarkably adept at moving freight—fortunately for their longevity. When the number of passenger trains—on the

Pennsy as around the country—began to decline, GG1's in increasing numbers were transferred to freight service, where they replaced the P5a's. Between April 1940 and June 1943, GG1's Nos. 4801 to 4844 were re-geared to pull freight. In 1952, Nos. 4827-4841 were geared back for passenger running; just two years later, however, most of these locomotives were once again geared for freight. By 1967, all GG1's from 4800 to 4881 had received 90-m.p.h. freight gearing. When hauling freight, the G's generally operate in pairs, though motors operated singly with light trains and "tripleheaders" are sometimes seen. But two GG1's can pull almost anything a yardmaster can hand them.

The passenger network traditionally plied by the GG1's is simplicity itself. The main trunk extends from New York's Penn Station to Zoo tower in Philadelphia (with just the eight-mile Perth Amboy and Woodbridge Branch—a connection to the New York and Long Branch at South Amboy—as an appendage). At Zoo, the route diverges, sending tracks west to Harrisburg and south to Washington. Simple enough: but add freight operations to the pattern and it becomes far more complex.

Freight from the New York City area is gathered across the Hudson in New Jersey—at Greenville or Harsimus Cove yards on the river, or Meadows Yard. After proceeding down the "Broad Way" through Jersey, traffic headed west leaves the main at Morrisville (just across the Delaware River into Pennsylvania) and continues on the Trenton Cutoff and the Philadelphia and Thorndale to Thorn tower, on the Philadelphia-Harrisburg main. Just eight miles further west, at Parkesburg, another route presents itself: the Atglen and Susquehanna, a low-grade freight line to Enola

Left: North of Columbia, Pa., a G-powered freight passes a pair of E44 rectifiers, among a fleet of 66 built by GE to replace the P5a's. Facing page, top left: Near Princeton Junction, N. J., a single G leads a short consist. KARL R. ZIMMERMANN

Facing page, top right: G's rest at Meadows engine terminal. STEVEN WARD

Facing page, bottom: A trio of G's work eastbound across the Delaware River at Trenton, N. J. TOM KELCEC

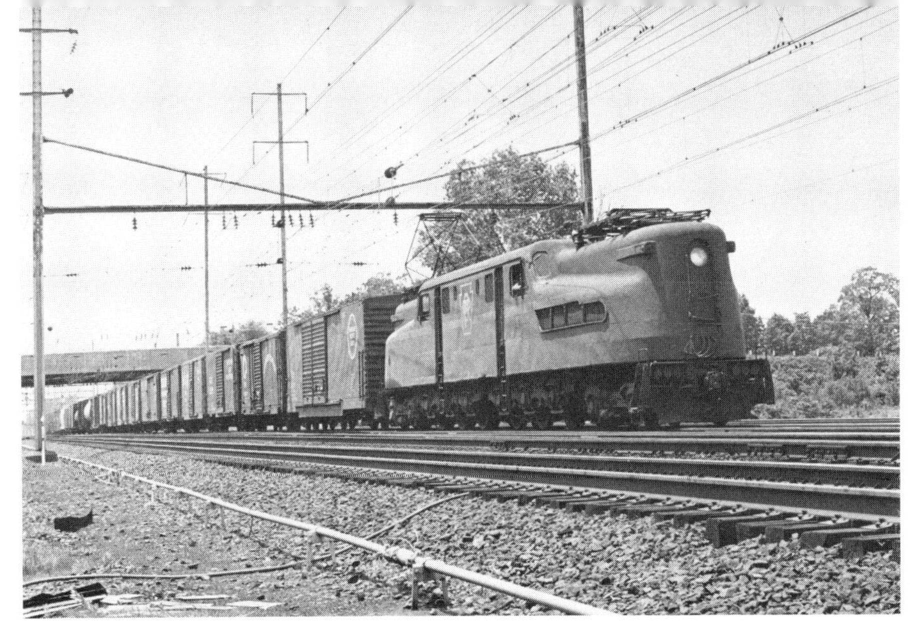

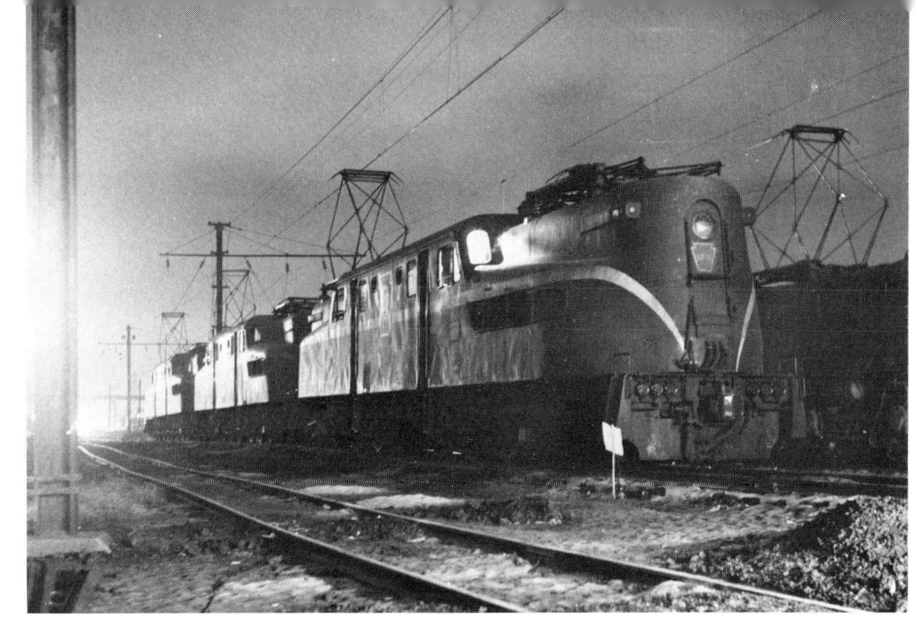

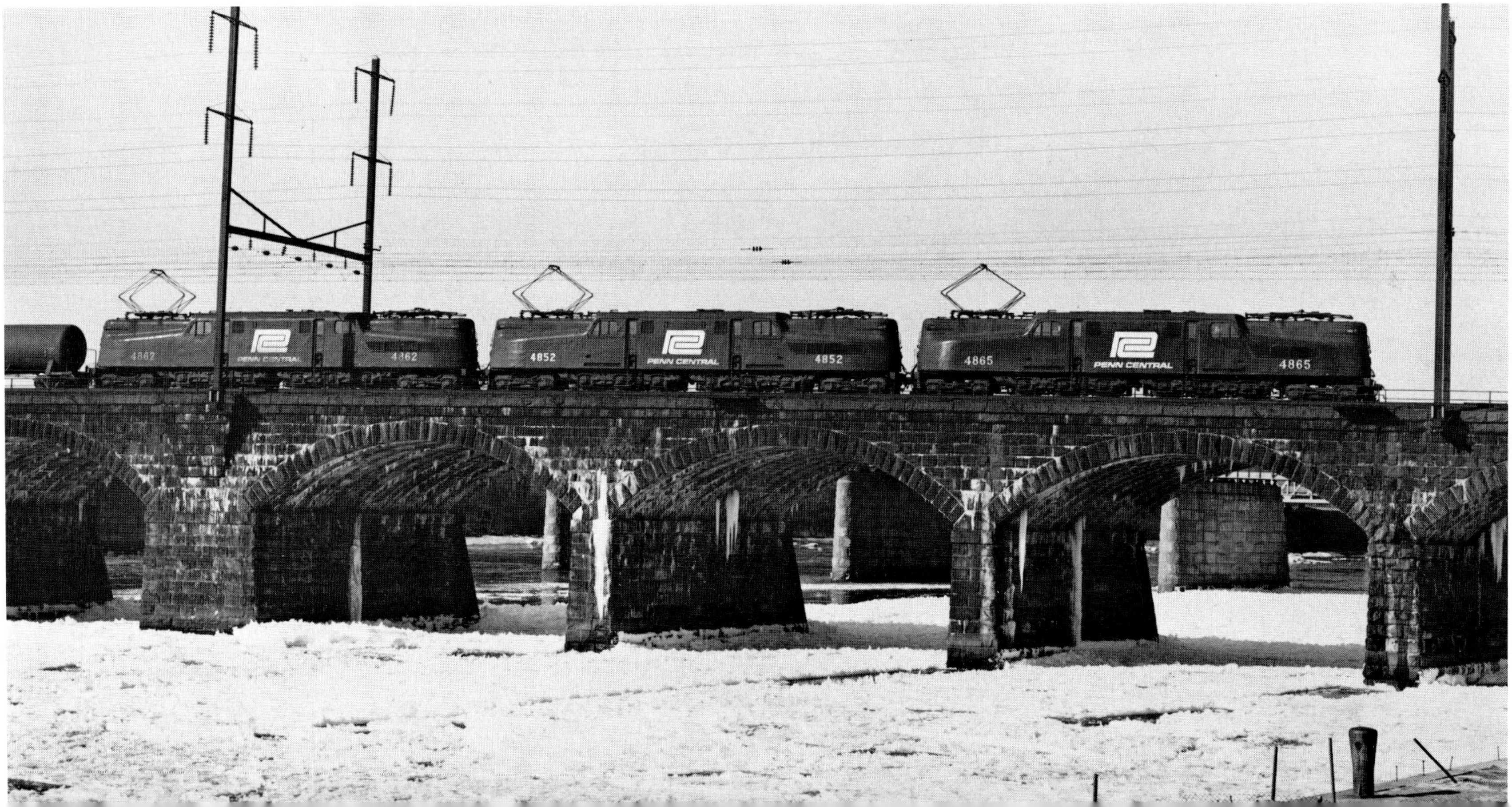
4862
PENN CENTRAL
4862
4852
PENN CENTRAL
4852
4865
PENN CENTRAL
4865

4839
PENNSYLVANIA
4839

Facing page: Speeding northbound near Edison, N. J., in 1963.
JIM SHAUGHNESSY

Right: Earnest Yard at Norristown, Pa., on October 19, 1963.
VICTOR HAND

Below: A solid Trans-American Trucking train from Cleveland highballs through Princeton Junction in May of 1966.
HERBERT H. HARWOOD, JR.

The Port Road

Left: *Southbound G's roll through Wildcat Tunnel on the Columbia and Port Deposit.* HOWARD SERIG

Right: *E44 rectifiers meet G's near Columbia in March 1975.* MAX ROBIN

Yard (on the west bank of the Susquehanna River, across from Harrisburg), via Columbia.

Traffic from Enola for Baltimore or points south heads out on the Atglen and Susquehanna, then gets on the Columbia and Port Deposit—the "Port Road"—and continues to follow the Susquehanna River to Perryville, the junction with the Philadelphia-Washington main. Providing further diverse routings is the Columbia Branch, which leaves the east-west main at Lancaster, drops down through Columbia, and rejoins the main 26 miles west at Royalton.

In the ex-PRR, ex-PC, now Conrail/Amtrak network under wire, there are numerous focal points; none is more interesting than Zoo Junction in Philadelphia. Here, presided over by a substantial brick tower which takes its name from the adjacent Philadelphia Zoo, freight and passenger trains to and from the west curve through the "Pittsburgh Subway"; passenger trains for the south head for

30th Street Station; M.U. service originating at Suburban Station—once all MP54's, now largely "Silverliners"—knots itself into the complex of routes here. Zoo also launches the West Philadelphia Elevated Branch—the "High Line" which allows north-south freight to bypass 30th Street Station. Both freight and passenger trains seem to fly by in all directions—beneath bridges, in and out of tunnels, along fills, and through cuts.

Another busy spot is Cola tower in Columbia, with freights banging by for the "Port Road," Atglen and Susquehanna, and Columbia Branch. The city of Baltimore is busy too—an inadvertent focus, a bottleneck. The culprit is the B&P tunnel, just south of the city's passenger station. (B&P stands for Baltimore and Potomac, the PRR subsidiary which built the Washington-Baltimore line.) Though Union Tunnel, just to the north of the station, was enlarged with a new bore during the electrification program, the B&P has remained untouched since 1873: a narrow, curving, two-

Left: G's roll north through the town of Columbia, with Cola tower in the background. KARL R. ZIMMERMANN

Right: Coal moves over the "Port Road" near Peach Bottom, Md. VICTOR HAND

Action at Zoo tower: A northbound freight has come off the "High Line" and rolls by the tower (above). Below, the New York section of the Broadway *emerges from the "Pittsburgh Subway" and is headed west (left); shortly thereafter, the Washington section appears (right).* KARL R. ZIMMERMANN

Facing page, top: "Tunnel helper" No. 4881 gets on a solid coal train in Bay View Yard. HERBERT H. HARWOOD, JR.

Facing page, bottom: Another busy spot is Newark Station. Here, a northbound Amtraker arrives. CHARLES CASSER

track tunnel. Furthermore, it is on a 1.4% gradient against westbound trains.

To move freight over this line, a full-time helper is assigned; in recent years, the GG1 has held down this job. The "tunnel helper" is based at the passenger station; it gets on the point of freights either there or at Bay View Yard, on the east side of town. The GG1 leads its train, which may be either electric or diesel powered, through the B&P tunnel and southwest to Gwynn Tower, seven miles from Bay View and three from Baltimore's Penn Station. At Gwynn, the helper's job is done; the motor cuts off and runs back to the station to await its next assignment. Standing there alone, the G is prominently visible to passengers aboard trains stopping at Baltimore.

The "Baltimore helper" assignment is not very glamorous compared to the GG1's early calling: high-speed passenger service exclusively. Though in performance capability the G's have changed

Action at B&P Junction in Baltimore: Above, train No. 549 leaves for Harrisburg via the Northern Central route through York, Pa., while "pigs" from "Pot Yard" emerge from the B&P Tunnel. Northbound (facing page, top left) and southbound (facing page, right) passenger trains move through the junction. Facing page, bottom left: A doubleheaded Washington-New York passenger train exits B&P Tunnel, passing the "tunnel helper." HERBERT H. HARWOOD, JR.

B&P Junction

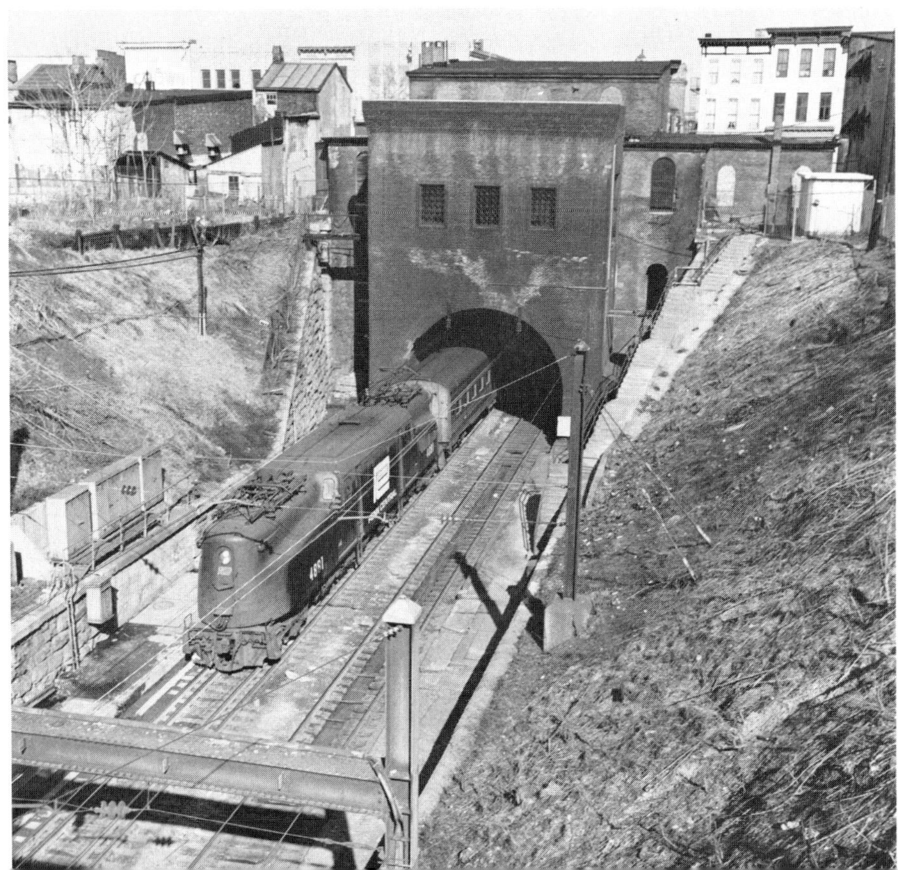

very little, circumstances have. Another thing that's changed over the years, and often, is the paint scheme applied to the GG1's. Even while the Pennsy was still the Pennsy there was a variety of liveries. No. 4800's original confused striping gave way almost immediately to the Loewy-originated five-stripe "cat's-whiskers" design—though the stripes were more widely spaced on No. 4800 than on all the production motors which followed. For his lettering and numerals, Loewy rejected the Clarendon style carried at the time by Pennsy steam power and substituted a very clean sans-serif Futura lettering, which he undoubtedly thought more compatible with the simplicity of his over-all conception. Lettering, numerals, and striping were in gold leaf; small keystones on each nose and high on each flank bore the locomotive's number. "PRR dark green"—also known as "Brunswick" green, and popularly described as being seven parts black and one part green—was then and continued through the Pennsy era to be the basic body color.

Beginning in August 1941 the traditional Pennsylvania lettering—the Clarendon style—came back into use on all PRR passenger cars and locomotives. No. 4875 was the first GG1 to be relettered in this way. Also at this time, the keystones on the GG1's sides began carrying the PRR monogram in a red field, rather than the locomotive number. In some cases the nose keystones too were changed in this manner.

Though green was the standard GG1 color, there were a few departures from it. In January of 1952, the PRR began painting six GG1's—Nos. 4908-4913— Tuscan red for use on the new Budd-built *Senator* and *Congressional* trains, put in service on March 17. The following year No. 4876, after being totally rebuilt following a wreck, was also put in the five-stripe red scheme, as were Nos. 4856, 4857, and 4929. Also in 1952, gold leaf was

Top left: Southbound at B&P Junction. Bottom left: A New York-Washingon train emerges from the B&P Tunnel at the long-abandoned Pennsylvania Avenue Station in Baltimore. HERBERT H. HARWOOD, JR.

Facing page, top: The original standard paint scheme.
RAYMOND LOEWY COLLECTION

Facing page, bottom: In this May 1937 view of train No. 271 at Elizabeth, N. J., GG1 No. 4829 shows a unique paint scheme, virtually unrecorded, in which the five narrow pinstripes merge into one.
GEORGE E. VOTAVA

4843 PENNSYLVANIA 4843

Above left: *Eastbound through Thorndale, Pa., in April 1954.* DON BALL, JR.

Above right: *Nos. 4871 and 4893 at Pennsylvania Station, New York.* JIM SHAUGHNESSY

Below: *G's began receiving the traditional Pennsy Clarendon lettering in 1941.* ALTOONA PUBLIC LIBRARY

Facing page: *No. 4863 works an eastbound passenger assignment at Lancaster in January 1955.* FRED W. SCHNEIDER, III

PENNSYLVANIA

4871
PENNSYLVANIA
4871

Left: *Heading north at Colonia, N.J.* ROGER COOK

Below: *Again at Colonia, this time southbound.* KARL R. ZIMMERMANN

Facing page: *No. 4871 strides through Elizabeth with authority.* DON WOOD

4936

4802
PENNSYLVANIA
4802

discontinued in all passenger car and locomotive striping and lettering and was replaced by Dupont's "Dulux"—a gold-colored synthetic.

In March 1955 came a dramatic change in the GG1's livery, ushered in by No. 4885. The five gold stripes became a single eight-inch yellow band; the red keystone on the side became many times larger and gained white monogramming and edging, plus black shadowing; the letters also grew considerably—to sixteen-inch Roman. Though the great generality of G's still wore dark green, two—Nos. 4907 and 4916—were dressed in Tuscan red and three—Nos. 4866, 4872, and 4880—in silver. This trio, intended for *Congressional* service, had broad red stripes and black lettering. All the off-color mavericks eventually wore "Brunswick" green again before going on to other liveries wrought by the corporate demise of the PRR.

The Pennsy's final paint scheme—the broad-stripe—was truly striking and projected a far more modern image than the subtle design it replaced. Nonetheless, the new scheme did still suggest the basic Loewy concepts of thirty years earlier: keystones front and side, striping tapering down at the noses, and lettering stretched broadly along the locomotive's flank. A subsequent simplification of the large keystones somewhat damaged the impact of this flashy scheme, which might in retrospect be called one of the last bold gestures the Pennsy made.

Facing page: G's after dark, being washed (left) and posing (bottom right) at Ivy City, the engine terminal for Washington, and at Sunnyside (top right), the yard for New York's Pennsylvania Station.
JIM SHAUGHNESSY

A most elusive paint scheme was the Pennsy's broad-stripe silver livery, worn by just three motors, and only briefly. No. 4866 is seen at Washington's Ivy City (top), and No. 4872 at North Philadelphia (middle) and Washington Union Station (bottom). The third locomotive to receive the silver scheme was No. 4880.

JIM EDMONSTON

FRANK TATNALL

H. L. BUCKLEY

Top left: No. 4902—wearing a one-of-a-kind blue and yellow paint scheme applied especially for the May 19, 1969 Baltimore-New York run which concluded the Golden Spike Centennial Limited's return trip from Ogden, Utah—waits in Baltimore for that call. TOM KELCEC

Bottom left: No. 4902, shown here running north at Colonia with a "Clocker," kept its blue "American Railroads" dress for a time. KARL R. ZIMMERMANN

Top right: No. 921—emerging from a swirl of snow at Metuchen, N. J. —also had a one-of-a-kind scheme: a huge United States Savings Bonds logo applied by Amtrak. ROGER COOK.

Facing page, bottom: The odd couple: No. 4801—the last G to lose pinstripes, in 1974—teams with No. 4836 to move PC freight through Baltimore. HOWARD SERIG

Facing page, top: TT1 awaits its departure for Chicago at Meadows Yard in 1960. Broad- and pinstripe pairings were common during the transition between schemes. DON WOOD

Whatever the paint job, the real story of the GG1 is its regular performance over a period of more than forty years: hauling passenger trains in excess of twenty cars at speeds up to one hundred miles per hour, day in and day out, with breakdowns hardly ever; lugging freight and lots of it from "Pot Yard" to Meadows, from Enola to Morrisville; rising to the unprecedented demands of traffic to and from Washington during World War II; aging so gracefully as to not seem older at all. For the GG1, it was the routine that was spectacular. Yet there inevitably were a number of dates and occasions that—in the diary of a locomotive—remain of uncommon interest to anyone who peruses its history.

April 20, 1939. The New York World's Fair opened, providing a showcase for GG1's Nos. 4888 and 4896, which were on display there in successive years in a Raymond Loewy-dominated setting. Not only was the Railroad Building a Loewy design, but so was the Chrysler Motors building, the focal exhibit of the Transportation Zone. No. 4896 was undoubtedly somewhat upstaged by No. 6100, Pennsy's huge one-of-a-kind S1, a 6-4-4-6 duplex passenger locomotive spectacularly streamlined by Loewy. The S1 steamed along at sixty miles per hour on a treadmill, going nowhere. The fair's theme was "Building the World of Tomorrow," and many of the exhibits seemed implausibly futuristic. Now, 38 years later, most of the developments hypothesized—super-highways and space flight, for instance—have become realities; some, such as the fair's Moderne architecture, are already passe. Yet the GG1, very much a reality in 1939, is still here today and still fresh-looking and functional.

July 20, 1948. The fact that the GG1 design was then 13 years old did not deter the Pennsy from showing No. 4912 at the Chicago Railroad Fair. For company, the GG1 had the PRR's Loewy-styled T1 4-4-4-4 duplex. And seven years later, in 1955, the GG1 was still being proudly exhibited. This time the motor was No. 4880, newly painted silver, and the occasion the "Parade of Progress" show in Baltimore, held for the National Model Railroad Association convention there by five area railroads, including the PRR.

January 15, 1953. Nothing is perfect, not even the GG1. On this day, No. 4876 was headed south toward Washington with the overnight *Federal* from Boston, when its brakes failed. The rampaging motor crashed through the bumping post at Union Station, blitzed the stationmaster's office and a newsstand, burst uninvited into the arched-ceilinged concourse, and sank through the floor. Fortunately, there were no fatalities—not even No. 4876, which was cut in pieces, hoisted from the basement, sent to Altoona for reassembling, and put back on the road again before year's end looking just the same as before the accident but for a new coat of red paint.

February, 1958. Freak weather caused the only significant blemish on the GG1 fleet's record of reliability. High winds and bitter cold created a snow fine in texture almost to the point of invisibility—and

Facing page, top: *No. 4896 at the New York World's Fair.*
SMITHSONIAN INSTITUTION

Facing page, middle: *No. 4912 at the Chicago Railroad Fair.*
JOHN KRAUSE

Facing page, bottom: *No. 4876 after the* Federal *accident.*
ARA MESROBIAN

Below: *G's generally took snow in stride, as here at Colonia.*
ROGER COOK

Right: *Cold weather often crippled the Metroliners; here, at New Brunswick, N. J., a G has come to the rescue.* TOM KELCEC

BETTER BE DEAD SURE
THAN SURE DEAD
PRR
4866
ENNSYLVANIA

Wilmington Shops

Wilmington Shops, now euphemistically known as the "Wilmington Maintenance Facility," is still the hospital for G's and is as busy as ever rewinding traction motors and welding main frames to keep the aging fleet—which currently numbers 106—on the road. Amtrak now owns the shops, but all GG1 maintenance—running repairs, monthly inspection, class repairs, and heavy mileage overhauls—is performed here for Conrail and New Jersey D. O. T. as well as Amtrak. The photos above left reflect the regearing that occurred as the G's went into freight service. All these photographs were taken in July 1967, though little but the color of the locomotives has changed in the decade since then. TOM KELCEC

Above: This strange animal, the remains of GG1 No. 4846, which was scrapped in 1967, is used as a self-propelled snow blower to clear the switches in the shop area at Wilmington. KARL R. ZIMMERMANN

fine enough to penetrate the French-linen filters on the GG1's air intakes. Once inside where it didn't belong, the snow melted and short-circuited the traction motors, disabling at one time or another virtually every locomotive in the fleet and thus causing the worst passenger-service failure in PRR history.

Chaos reigned for days. At one point more than seventy G's were down; as fast as Wilmington Shops could fix them, more cripples appeared requiring repairs. P5a's led disabled GG1's around by the nose, the G's being left in the consist only to provide steam heat. One particular day less than a third of the New York-Philadelphia trains operated, and delays were common over an extended period. Diesels were brought in from throughout the PRR system and from some southern roads, which were exempt from these cold-weather miseries. In effect, Manhattan Transfer was reborn as a locomotive exchange point, as diesels were traded for electric power in the

Jersey Meadows.

In the aftermath of this monumental tie-up, the Pennsy took steps to assure that such a crisis would not occur again. In analyzing why the GG1's had proven so much more susceptible than the P5's to the powdered snow, the Pennsy concluded that the fine crystals formed at just that level above the ground at which the GG1's air intakes were placed; the P5's, with higher intakes, were not affected. Therefore, the railroad instituted a program to relocate the intakes to a position just below the pantographs. This alteration—eventually made to approximately forty motors, mostly the newer ones—was the only major change ever imposed on the original Loewy styling. Though a practical necessity, it was an aesthetic liability. Two designs were used, one of them particularly oversized and boxy. In any case, the cure apparently worked, as the problem has not recurred since.

Facing page, bottom: A pair of GG1's and an ex-New Haven EP5 await assignment in the engine terminal at Morrisville, Pa., in March 1976. The "modern" EP5's, introduced in 1955, never could match the G's, which have outlived them. KARL R. ZIMMERMANN

The Penn Central merger introduced GG1's to the Hell Gate Bridge on runs to New Haven, such as the Springfield-bound Connecticut Yankee *(above) and Boston-bound* Bay State *(below).* VICTOR HAND

March 3, 1966. Nos. 4804, 4831, and 4847 were retired, the first GG1's to leave the roster. This was the initial certain and irrefutable evidence that even GG1's could not last forever, and it began an accelerating series of retirements. Still, in the course of the next decade only thirty additional motors fell to the scrappers, leaving in 1976 a full three-quarters of the roster intact, at ages ranging from 33 to 42 years.

October 29, 1967. The Pennsy's fall timetables for the Northeast Corridor listed the GG1-hauled *Afternoon Congressionals* at three hours and twenty minutes between New York and Washington with six stops—the best carded time ever. (During World War II, advance sections of the *Congressional* had made the run non-stop

No. 4935, famous nine years later as the locomotive restored by "Friends of the GG1," in 1968 is simply an alien among FL9's in New Haven (top left). Under unique NYNH&H catenary, G's pull The Minute Man *at Noroton Heights (bottom left) and* The Murray Hill *at Cos Cob draw (bottom right).* DON BALL, JR.

in just over three hours.) The fall 1967 carding was achieved by raising the speed limit in some places from 80 to 100 miles per hour.

Ironically, it was a program designed to displace the G's from their preeminent position in passenger hauling that gave the motors this chance to strut their stuff at the fastest speeds ever. The High Speed Ground Transportation Act of 1965 established government cooperation with the PRR in upgrading the Washington-New York corridor and designing new high-speed trains to serve it—which turned out to be the Metroliners. Though these multiple-unit speedsters were expected to enter service in the fall of 1967, repeated mechanical problems kept them sidetracked until more than a year after that.

Meanwhile, the lid was off the G's, and 100-mile-per-hour run-

After the PC merger, GG1's were common in New Haven; a G-powered New Englander *passes Nos. 910 and 4936 on the motor track (bottom left). On the ex-Pennsy electrified main, the coming of PC meant little for the GG1's, shown meeting at Colonia (top) and pulling a "Clocker" at Metropark (bottom right).* KARL R. ZIMMERMANN

Top right: The Kennedy funeral train at Elizabeth, N. J. TOM KELCEC

Top left: Many hours later, far off schedule, the funeral train at Baltimore. HERBERT H. HARWOOD, JR.

Bottom: From Pennsy to PC to Conrail and New Jersey D. O. T.—G's have long handled trains bound for the New York and Long Branch. In this view, No. 1168 is eastbound at Perth Amboy in 1972.
VICTOR HAND

ning had the company's blessing. A special instruction booklet was published, listing all the passenger cars approved for 100-m.p.h. operation: not only PRR, but also Seaboard Air Line, Atlantic Coast Line, Seaboard Coast Line (some cars already renumbered after the recent merger), Southern, Chesapeake and Ohio, Baltimore and Ohio, Richmond, Fredericksburg and Potomac, and Louisville and Nashville. While it lasted—and it only did for a few months—this fast running once again amply demonstrated the G's extraordinary potentialities.

February 1, 1968. On this day the Penn Central was born, and the Pennsy became only a memory. For the GG1's, this meant the gradual application of a new paint scheme. "Brunswick" green, striping, and keystones gave way to unaesthetic, unadorned black with awkward, intertwined "PC"—the "mating worms." Most of the G's came to wear small PC logos on their noses and large ones across their sides, with "Penn Central" written out beneath. On a few of the motors, the broad yellow stripe from the PRR scheme was retained, and a small "PC" placed below it. In addition, a few motors bore an experimental scheme featuring two-color "worms."

When the New Haven was included in the PC merger on January 1, 1969, the GG1 gained a new sphere of operations—the 75-mile Hell Gate Bridge route from Penn Station in New York to New Haven. Back in 1964, the G's had been tested on the NYNH&H for clearances and power compatibility and found acceptable. From 1969 on, there were no locomotive changes necessary at Penn Station, and GG1's became a familiar sight in New Haven.

One good turn deserves another. Above: On October 14, 1969, No. 4857 hauls The Flying Scotsman *under New Haven catenary at New Rochelle, N. Y., during the British locomotive's visit to this country; the G is present to bring the train into Penn Station in New York.* JOHN KRAUSE

Below: On December 14, 1976, Strasburg Rail Road's 2-6-0 No. 89 trundles a crippled Conrail GG1 through Carpenter's, Pa. No. 4855 had burned out a truck bearing at Parkesburg, Pa., and was being moved to the Strasburg's drop table for repair. This was the second occasion on which the little Strasburg had come to a giant G's rescue in this fashion, though in the first instance—in October 1974—a diesel did the honors. JOHN J. BOWMAN, JR.

Amtrak
906

Amtrak
904

902
Amtrak
902

Facing page, top left: Though Amtrak retained the PC black on most of its GG1's, six motors—Nos. 905, 906, 909, 924, 926, and 927—received a platinum mist, red, and blue scheme. No. 906 roars through the snow at Metuchen leading The Montrealer. ROGER COOK

Facing page, top right: Amtrak introduced passenger service to the "Port Road." Here the Washington section of The Broadway Limited *is westbound at Peach Bottom, Md., on a July 1975 afternoon.*
VICTOR HAND

Facing page, bottom: An eastbound "Clocker" at Metuchen. Right: The National Limited's *Washington section, which operates tri-weekly, is most often a single coach. On July 10, 1976, the consist rolling through Holtwood, Pa. on the Susquehanna River is twice that size.*
KARL R. ZIMMERMANN

June 8, 1968. This was an occasion for which the otherwise too-somber PC black was appropriate: Robert Kennedy's funeral train from New York to Washington. Behind Nos. 4901 and 4903 came a 21-car consist, ending with PC open-platform business car No. 120—the "Pennsylvania," though nameless on this occasion—which bore the late senator's body. Running ahead was a three-car pilot train led by GG1 No. 4932; Nos. 4900 and 4910 followed light as protection power.

At Elizabeth, N. J., a second tragedy was piled on the first. Crowds pushed out on the northbound tracks for a better view as the special approached. *The Admiral* from Chicago rounded the bend, 25 miles per hour below allowed speed, with horn blaring and bell ringing. Nonetheless, by the time the crowd's attention was drawn from the funeral train to *The Admiral's* GG1, it was too late for everyone to scramble off the tracks. The toll: two dead and another four injured. After that the PC agreed to stop all train movements around the special.

The funeral train had left New York about half an hour late and lost another four hours en route because of the crowds at track-side. Nos. 4901 and 4903 finally nosed into Washington Union Station at 9:08 p.m., ending a sad and costly venture.

May 1, 1971. Amtrak's assumption of most of the nation's passenger service, which occurred on this date, has had numerous ramifications for the GG1's. At first the changes to the motors wrought by the quasi-governmental passenger corporation were purely cosmetic. On the forty GG1's that Amtrak eventually would own, the "mating worms" were replaced by a simple "Amtrak" in the corporation's Helvetica style. Six motors received a red, blue, and platinum mist scheme somewhat reminiscent of the silver G's of the mid-Fifties; the others remained black, some with the yellow stripe.

Amtrak has renumbered its GG1's in a generally perplexing fashion. It has created a 900-929 series—which represents the initial 30 locomotives purchased—apparently by simply dropping the first digit of the original number. However, in only five of the thirty cases do the numbers actually correlate this way. In addition, Amtrak at the close of 1976 rostered ten GG1's with four-digit numbers. In five instances the numbers were original; the other five were renumberings, including one anomaly: 4939, which had never been a GG1 number, since the series stopped at 4938.

Facing page, top: The past, present, and future of electrification on the Northeast Corridor are all in evidence as a GG1 pulls an E60 and the diminutive ASEA-built Swedish Rc-4 electric which Amtrak brought to the United States on a trial lease in 1976. Subsequently, a French electric was also tested. ROGER COOK

Facing page, bottom: Approximately fifty G's remain active hauling freight for Conrail; among them are Nos. 4806 and 4855, seen here working south through Metuchen on a bright fall morning in 1976. Above: The "tunnel helper" from Baltimore leads a dead E60 across the Susquehanna at Perryville, Md. KARL R. ZIMMERMANN

Under Amtrak's aegis GG1's began hauling passenger trains down the "Port Road"—something they had not done while wearing keystones, since Washington-Harrisburg trains traditionally took the non-electrified Northern Central route through York, Pa. At first, the Washington sections of both the *Broadway Limited* to Chicago and the *National Limited* to Kansas City used the Columbia and Port Deposit north from Perryville. Later, the *Broadway* was rerouted through Philadelphia, leaving only the one- or two-coach *National* on the highly scenic "Port Road."

Of course, Amtrak's most significant action regarding the GG1's has been to replace them—at least in part—with a fleet of 26 E60CP rectifiers from General Electric. The circumstances surrounding the introduction of these rather ungainly C-C electrics were enough to make a GG1 fan smirk: the first E60, No. 950, derailed during tests on February 24, 1975. Investigators determined the problem to be lack of stability in the trucks at high speed, a conclusion which GE rejected. In any case, the Federal Railway Administration put the E60's on the shelf pending truck redesign or modification; they didn't come off until late November, and then with permission to run only 85 miles per hour.

So the GG1's had a nine-month reprieve; eventually, however, the E60's were all running—albeit with fairly frequent breakdowns at first. Proponents of the theory that history repeats itself point to parallels between the E60's and the P5's of forty years earlier: both experienced severe tracking problems, and both were initially built in the box-cab style, affording no protection for the engine crew. Neither was wholly successful, and both left their owners looking for something better. In 1934, that meant the GG1. In the late 1970's, it will very likely mean a locomotive of foreign manufacture, or at least design, since there has been little ongoing development of electric locomotives with high-speed potential in the United States in recent years.

April 1, 1976. The advent of Conrail had little immediate effect on the PC's fleet of GG1's in freight service, other than that the letters "CR" replaced "PC" on the motors' dusty black sides and noses. Throughout 1976, power-short Conrail kept the G's rolling; as the year ended, no locomotives were on order to replace them, nor were there any firm plans in that direction.

How large a future does the GG1 actually have? One factor assumed to work strongly against its longevity is Amtrak's and Conrail's desire to convert their operations under wire from 11,000-volt, 25-cycle to 25,000-volt, 60-cycle current. This change would allow the railroad to tap directly into commercial power grids, eliminating the need for expensive frequency converter stations. Only the GG1's stand in the way of the change, since virtually all other equipment in service—the ex-Virginian E33 and ex-PRR E44 freighters, the Metroliners, the Silverliner suburban M.U. cars, and the E60's—are rectifiers and convertable to the new line voltage.

As 1977 began, however, things were not looking entirely bleak for the GG1. Plans for the conversion were still not firm; in fact, Amtrak and Conrail officials were rumored to have developed serious reservations about it. Also on the positive side, Amtrak still

had 40 GG1's on the roster, Conrail 53, and the New Jersey Department of Transportation 13, for their North Jersey Coast trains. No locomotives were on order to replace any of these. Furthermore, an unusual seige of bitterly cold weather had ushered in the new year. Amtrak's Corridor services were in disarray, as were its operations throughout most of the country. While E60's and Metroliners succumbed to snow, ice, and cold, the G's kept running; some experienced observers suggested that, without the GG1's, Amtrak would have had to shut the Corridor down.

So there was life in the locomotives yet. On the other hand, age has been telling increasingly on the fleet of GG1's, particularly in the fatigue and corrosion of the locomotives' main frames. When all things are weighed, some GG1's can be expected to operate into the early 1980's, but probably not far beyond that. Amtrak, at any rate, had specific projections in its "Five-Year Plan" announced in late 1976 for their retirement at that time.

After years of being taken for granted, the GG1 by early 1977 began attracting renewed attention. One happy indication of this was the formation of a group called "Friends of the GG1," organized under National Railway Historical Society auspices. Its purpose was to restore a GG1 to its original livery of "Brunswick" green, keystones, and pinstripes, thus memoralizing Raymond Loewy's timeless design, the long, proud history of the Pennsylvania Railroad, and the G's extraordinary record of reliability over a 42-year period. Howard Serig, a rail buff and U. S. Department of Transportation economist, gave the project its first exposure through a "Turntable" opinion column in the November 1976 *Trains* magazine. In January, Serig convened a "Friends of the GG1" committee.

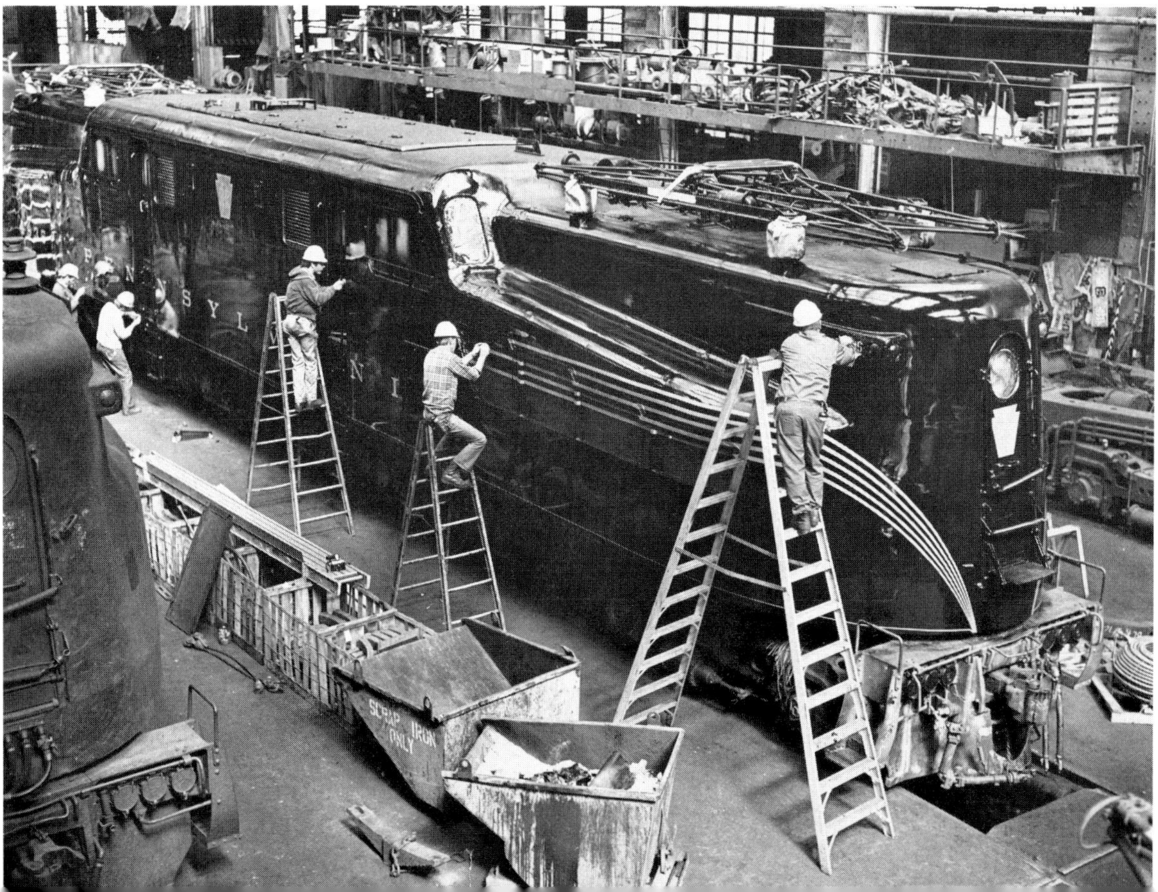

On May 1, 1977, at Wilmington Shops, "Friends of the GG1" locomotive No. 4935 is painted green, and then the masking tape is removed. KARL R. ZIMMERMANN

TOM KELCEC

Fund raising was begun, and Amtrak—having sanctioned the project—selected the motor to be restored: No. 4935, the only Amtrak G with unmodified air intake louvres and its original number.

On March 9, Amtrak and the committee signed a formal agreement. Within two weeks, 4935 was in Wilmington Shops and work had begun. The locomotive was sandblasted and primed; it then received extensive carbody renewal, which involved outright replacement of much metal sheeting and, elsewhere, the filling in of dents with putty. (Concurrently, Amtrak performed considerable mechanical and electrical work on the locomotive at its own expense to insure its longevity. The purely cosmetic work was paid for by the "Friends of the GG1"—with check #4935 in the amount of $8,712.) Next the locomotive's shell was undercoated; the red for the keystones and gold for the stripes and lettering were applied and masked with tape meticulously cut from original stencils.

Sunday, May 1, was a memorable day at Wilmington Shops, for on this occasion the "Brunswick" green—Dupont's "Dulux" paint, like the other colors—was applied to No. 4935, and the masking removed. For this latter task, a delicate one, most of the small weekend shift from throughout the locomotive shop appeared. As lettering, keystones, striping, and cat's whiskers materialized, the excitement grew. Everyone wore broad smiles, and congratulated each other. Suddenly all the tape was off and 4935—now essentially restored—stood bathed in bright sunshine pouring through the grimy skylights.

On Wednesday, May 11, these men who actually performed the restoration were honored in a brief dedication ceremony at Wilmington Shops. The following day, 4935 ran light to Perryville, Md., to test its renewed mechanical and electrical systems. No problems developed. On Saturday, Raymond Loewy—honorary chairman of "Friends of the GG1" and guest of honor at the upcoming formal dedication—rode from New York to Washington with committee members aboard George and Anita Pins's *Pennsylvania,* No. 120, once the PRR's premier business car. At Washington, No. 120 was joined by Larry Battley's *Lionel-Ives* (formerly PRR *Alder Falls*); both cars wear authentic Pennsy Tuscan and gold and thus were a perfect complement for No. 4935.

At noon on Sunday, May 15, before a gathering of approximately 300 at Washington Union Station, the dedication ceremony began under brilliantly blue skies. Serig opened the program and was followed on No. 120's observation platform—the perfect rostrum—by Raymond Loewy, Amtrak president Paul Reistrup, and this author. In the climactic event, Mrs. Reistrup broke a bottle of Pennsylvania champagne over 4935's pilot, after speaking these words: "To the Pennsylvania Railroad, 'The Standard Railroad of the World,' in honor of the men and women who worked for her and their service to the nation, I christen thee 'Pennsylvania 4935.' "

Then all that remained was for engineer Harry Wilgris, a 36-year veteran (who thus had two years' seniority on his GG1), to make a perfect run to New York with No. 4935 on *The Murray Hill,* and for thousands at trackside to watch, photograph, and hail the rebirth. After this inaugural run, No. 4935 reentered Amtrak's locomotive pool to begin writing yet another important chapter in the GG1 story.

In the unstable world of Eastern railroading in modern times, the GG1 has been one immutable value, something very special. The G has had an exemplary safety record, chiefly because of its excellent tracking characteristics. It is fast and powerful, and rarely breaks down. It was the first streamlined electric locomotive and maybe the handsomest ever. In 1976, Raymond Loewy would say this: "If we had to redesign it today, after forty years, I don't know what I would change. I would probably not change anything."

Above: The shop force poses at the May 11 gathering at Wilmington. Facing page: On May 15, 1977, the "Friends of the GG1" project came to a successful culmination. As the crowd gathered for the ceremony, a band played bluegrass music on No. 120's observation platform (top left). A proud Raymond Loewy posed with his new old engine (top right). Mrs. Reistrup christened 4935 with a bottle of Pennsylvania champagne (bottom left). At the end of a great day, No. 4935 raced out of the setting sun with The Murray Hill, *minutes away from an on-time arrival at New York.*

DON WOOD

KARL R. ZIMMERMANN

KEN MURRY

DON BALL, JR.

Roster

As of January 1, 1977

Number	Built	By	Disposition
4800	8/34	Bald./West.	CR
4801	5/35	GE	CR
4802	5/35	GE	CR
4803	6/35	GE	CR
4804	6/35	GE	ret. 3/66
4805	6/35	GE	ret. 1/68
4806	6/35	GE	CR
4807	6/35	GE	ret. 3/67
4808	7/35	GE	CR
4809	7/35	GE	CR
4810	7/35	GE	ret. 7/69
4811	7/35	GE	CR
4812	7/35	GE	ret. 10/66
4813	7/35	GE	ret. 3/67
4814	8/35	GE	ret. 3/67
4815	4/35	Bald./PRR/West.	CR
4816	5/35	Bald./PRR/West.	ret. 4/68
4817	5/35	Bald./PRR/GE	ret. 3/67
4818	5/35	Bald./PRR/GE	ret. 3/70
4819	5/35	Bald./PRR/West.	ret. 3/67
4820	5/35	Bald./PRR/West.	ret. 1/68
4821	5/35	Bald./PRR/West.	CR
4822	6/35	Bald./PRR/GE	CR
4823	6/35	Bald./PRR/West.	ret. 2/67
4824	6/35	Bald./PRR/Wes.	CR
4825	6/35	Bald./PRR/West.	CR
4826	6/35	Bald./PRR/West.	ret. 4/69
4827	6/35	Bald./PRR/West.	ret. 7/69
4828	6/35	Bald./PRR/West.	CR
4829	6/35	Bald./PRR/West.	ret. 4/67
4830	6/35	Bald./PRR/West.	ret. 2/67
4831	6/35	Bald./PRR/GE	ret. 3/66
4832	6/35	Bald./PRR/West.	ret. 3/70
4833	6/35	Bald./PRR/West.	ret. 10/66
4834	7/35	Bald./PRR/West.	ret. 11/67
4835	7/35	Bald./PRR/West.	CR
4836	7/35	Bald./PRR/West.	CR
4837	7/35	Bald./PRR/GE	ret. 4/68
4838	7/35	Bald./PRR/West.	CR
4839	7/35	Bald./PRR/West.	ret. 12/68
4840	4/35	PRR/West.	CR
4841	4/35	PRR/West.	CR
4842	4/35	PRR/West.	ret. 4/69
4843	5/35	PRR/West.	ret. 4/67
4844	5/35	PRR/West.	CR
4845	5/35	PRR/West.	ret. 8/75
4846	5/35	PRR/West.	ret. 3/67
4847	5/35	PRR/West.	ret. 3/66
4848	5/35	PRR/West.	CR
4849	5/35	PRR/GE	CR
4850	5/35	PRR/West.	CR
4851	6/35	PRR/West.	CR
4852	6/35	PRR/West.	CR
4853	6/35	PRR/West.	CR
4854	6/35	PRR/West.	CR
4855	6/35	PRR/GE	CR
4856	6/35	PRR/GE	CR
4857	6/35	PRR/West.	CR
4858	10/37	PRR/GE	CR
4859	12/37	PRR/GE	CR
4860	12/37	PRR/GE	CR
4861	12/37	PRR/GE	CR
4862	12/37	PRR/GE	CR
4863	1/38	PRR/West.	CR
4864	1/38	PRR/West.	CR
4865	1/38	PRR/West.	CR
4866	1/38	PRR/West.	ret. 8/75
4867	1/38	PRR/West.	CR
4868	2/38	PRR/West.	CR
4869	12/38	PRR/West.	CR
4870	12/38	PRR/West.	CR
4871	12/38	PRR/GE	ret. 8/67
4872	1/39	PRR/West.	NJDOT
4873	1/39	PRR/GE	NJDOT
4874	1/39	PRR/West.	NJDOT
4875	1/39	PRR/GE	NJDOT
4876	1/39	PRR/West.	NJDOT
4877	1/39	PRR/West.	NJDOT
4878	2/39	PRR/GE	NJDOT
4879	2/39	PRR/West.	NJDOT
4880	2/39	PRR/GE	NJDOT
4881	2/39	PRR/GE	NJDOT
4882	2/39	PRR/GE	NJDOT
4883	3/39	PRR/West.	NJDOT
4884	3/39	PRR/GE	NJDOT
4885	3/39	PRR/West.	CR
4886	3/39	PRR/GE	CR
4887	4/39	PRR/GE	CR
4888	4/39	PRR/West.	ret. 8/67
4889	3/40	PRR/West.	CR
4890	3/40	PRR/GE	AMT
4891	4/40	PRR/West.	CR
4892	3/40	PRR/GE	AMT 900
4893	4/40	PRR/West.	AMT
4894	4/40	PRR/GE	CR
4895	4/40	PRR/West.	AMT
4896	4/40	PRR/GE	AMT
4897	4/40	PRR/West.	AMT 901
4898	5/40	PRR/GE	CR
4899	5/40	PRR/West.	AMT 902
4900	5/40	PRR/GE	AMT 903
4901	5/40	PRR/West.	AMT 904
4902	5/40	PRR/GE	AMT 905
4903	6/40	PRR/West.	AMT 906
4904	6/40	PRR/GE	AMT 4930
4905	8/40	PRR/West.	AMT 4931
4906	6/40	PRR/GE	AMT 907
4907	8/40	PRR/West.	AMT 908
4908	7/40	PRR/GE	AMT 909
4909	12/41	PRR/GE	AMT 4932
4910	12/41	PRR/GE	AMT 910
4911	1/42	PRR/GE	AMT 911
4912	1/42	PRR/GE	AMT 912
4913	1/42	PRR/GE	AMT 913
4914	6/42	PRR/GE	AMT 914
4915	6/42	PRR/West.	AMT 4933
4916	6/42	PRR/GE	AMT 915
4917	6/42	PRR/West.	CR 4934
4918	7/42	PRR/GE	AMT 916
4919	7/42	PRR/West.	AMT 917
4920	7/42	PRR/GE	AMT 918
4921	7/42	PRR/West.	CR
4922	8/42	PRR/GE	CR
4923	8/42	PRR/GE	AMT 4938
4924	8/42	PRR/GE	AMT 919
4925	8/42	PRR/West.	AMT 920
4926	9/42	PRR/West.	AMT 921
4927	9/42	PRR/GE	AMT 4939
4928	10/42	PRR/West.	AMT 922
4929	2/43	PRR/West.	AMT 923
4930	2/43	PRR/West.	ret. 10/68
4931	2/43	PRR/West.	AMT 924
4932	3/43	PRR/GE	AMT 925
4933	3/43	PRR/West.	AMT 926
4934	3/43	PRR/GE	AMT 927
4935	4/43	PRR/GE	AMT
4936	4/43	PRR/GE	ret. 4/71
4937	4/43	PRR/West.	AMT 928
4938	6/43	PRR/GE	AMT 929

Bald. = Baldwin Locomotive Works
West. = Westinghouse Electric & Manufacturing Co.
GE = General Electric
PRR = Pennsylvania Railroad's Altoona Works
AMT = Amtrak
CR = Conrail
NJDOT = New Jersey Department of Transportation
ret. = Retired

Bibliography

"Big Saturday," *The Pennsy,* IV (January 1955), 8-10.

Bruno, M. L. "Passenger Extras to Philadelphia," *NRHS Bulletin,* (fourth quarter 1963), 32-38.

Burgess, George H. and Kennedy, Miles C. *Centennial History of the Pennsylvania Railroad Company.* Philadelphia: The Pennsylvania Railroad Company, 1949.

Chesley, Alan B. and Koester, Tony. "The Enduring GG1," *Railroad Model Craftsman,* XLIV (December 1975), 52-61 and (January 1976), 59-62.

"Electric Operation Opens Between Great American Cities — Capital and Metropolis Linked," *Train Talks,* (March 1935), unpaged.

Kalmbach, A. C. "Epoch of Electrification," *Trains,* VI (April 1946), 40-47.

Loewy, Raymond. Interview with the author, December 1976.

Loewy, Raymond. *Never Leave Well Enough Alone.* New York: Simon and Schuster, 1951.

Middleton, William D. *When the Steam Roads Electrified.* Milwaukee: Kalmbach Publishing Company, 1974.

Morgan, David P. "The Most Closely Watched Train," *Trains,* XXVIII (August 1968), 10-13.

The Pennsylvania Railroad Electrification. East Pittsburgh, Pa.: Westinghouse Electric and Manufacturing Company, 1936.

Pennypacker, Bert. "The Fabulous GG1 versus the E60CP," *Rails Northeast,* IV (September 1976), 8-15.

Staufer, Alvin F. *Pennsy Power.* Medina, Ohio: Alvin F. Staufer, 1962.

Staufer, Alvin F. and Pennypacker, Bert. *Pennsy Power II.* Medina, Ohio: Alvin F. Staufer, 1968.

Taylor, Joshua C. "Foreward," *The Designs of Raymond Loewy.* Washington, D.C.: Smithsonian Institution Press, 1975.

Westing, Frederick. "GG1," *Trains,* XXIV (March 1964), 20-36.